Praise for

THE ULTIMATE COMEBACK

"Authors Erik Kramer and William Croyle unfold a gripping, well-written, deeply heartfelt, and emotional story. Kramer describes his battle with depression so well that readers can understand what depression can cause in a person's psyche. *The Ultimate Comeback* is a powerful short read that packs so much insight and education about depression."

—READERS' FAVORITE BOOK REVIEWS

"Erik was a great competitor and a gifted quarterback. I enjoyed being his teammate and all of the guys respected him. I'm proud to see what Erik's doing with his second chance at life. This book will help a lot of people."

—BARRY SANDERS, DETROIT LIONS RUNNING BACK (1989-98), NFL MVP (1997), TEN-TIME PRO BOWLER, AND PRO FOOTBALL HALL OF FAME INDUCTEE (2004)

"The fall and rise—the inspirational rise—of Erik Kramer is a testament to his incredible spirit and candor. We all struggle in life, but I dare say Erik Kramer's struggles were ten times any of mine—and Erik has come out the other side with a purpose and a story that can help thousands. Truly, thanks to him for telling a story that will save lives."

—PETER KING, THREE-TIME NATIONAL SPORTS MEDIA ASSOCIATION SPORTSWRITER OF THE YEAR, AUTHOR, AND COLUMNIST FOR NBCSPORTS.COM

"I first met Erik in 1992 when he was leading the Detroit Lions to their best playoff finish in the Super Bowl era. He later joined the Chicago Bears, where he is still the team's season leader in passing yards and touchdowns. Along the way, he introduced me to his new baby son, Griffen, and I always thought to myself about Erik, *This guy is different from any pro quarterback I've met.*

"He was intelligent, reserved, thoughtful, empathetic, sincere, and somehow—it's hard to describe this beyond a feeling I had—suffering badly. Not physically, though—like all NFL quarterbacks, he'd been beaten aplenty on the football field—but mentally. I sensed it. Like the weight of many worlds was on his shoulders. Where was his joy?

"With this book, I now understand so much more about Erik and his struggles. His story is almost literally unbelievable. Yet it's true. It is a riveting tale of effort, success, failure, self-destruction, and rebirth. It is both heartbreaking and heart-warming, terrible and heroic. Ultimately, it is about the eternal quest for love—of friends, family, self, and, yes, life itself. There is no way to read *The Ultimate Comeback* and not feel your own life change or to wish only the best for Erik Kramer forever."

—RICK TELANDER, *CHICAGO SUN-TIMES* SENIOR SPORTS COLUMNIST AND
FORMER *SPORTS ILLUSTRATED* SENIOR WRITER

"I covered Erik as a player and sat beside him on television as a teammate, but after reading this book, I now know that I didn't know Erik at all. But neither did he. I'm in awe of Erik's vulnerability, sharing his story with the world, and turning his pain into purpose. It is heartbreaking, heart lifting, and so very inspirational. So many will read these words and find courage—and hope."

—LAURA OKMIN, *NFL ON FOX* SIDELINE REPORTER, AUTHOR, AND FOUNDER OF GALVANIZE

"I've known Erik Kramer for thirty-plus years, and I don't think I've been prouder of him. He has turned one of the darkest moments in his life into a story of triumph, courage, and incredible perseverance. *The Ultimate Comeback* shows us all things are possible. As men, we don't often talk about our mental health. Erik has reminded us that seeking help is not a sign of weakness, but an act of strength!"

—RODNEY PEETE, NFL QUARTERBACK (1989-2004), AUTHOR,
AND COHOST OF *ROGGIN AND RODNEY* ON AM 570 RADIO, LOS ANGELES

"Comeback stories dominate the games we love, but Erik Kramer's comeback is about life itself. I loved his football résumé, but his winning battle against the darker demons is what makes his story a great read."

—BRENT MUSBURGER, FORMER CBS, ABC, AND ESPN BROADCASTER AND
SPORTS EMMY LIFETIME ACHIEVEMENT AWARD WINNER

"Erik Kramer was known for his comebacks in the NFL, but nothing compares to what he's gone through—and returned from—in life. This is an engrossing read and one of the most compelling and important stories you'll ever read."

—DAN WETZEL, *NEW YORK TIMES* BEST-SELLING AUTHOR
AND *YAHOO SPORTS* NATIONAL COLUMNIST

"Erik was a prized free agent, signing during my tenure with the Bears, and lived up to expectations as a record-setting quarterback, team leader, and teammate. His book is a story that will be very impactful. He bears his soul on overcoming many challenges, and his account of his life after his playing days will serve as a tremendous inspiration to many people. I'm so proud of his courage to tell his story."

—DAVE WANNSTEDT, NFL AND NCAA COACH (1975-2013), CHICAGO BEARS HEAD COACH (1993-98), AND SUPER BOWL CHAMPION (XXVII)

"Perseverance through the lows and humility through the highs. EK has experienced both and is standing strong with a drive to impact people facing challenges similar to his own. Our coach used to say, 'What we give will grow; what we keep we lose.' EK is living those words."

—CHRIS SPIELMAN, NFL LINEBACKER (1988-97), FOUR-TIME PRO BOWLER, AND MEMBER OF THE DETROIT LIONS 75TH ANNIVERSARY TEAM

"EK's story is tragic and miraculous all at the same time. A mind-opening read. Erik has been a great support as I battled my own demons of depression. His recollections hit close to home, and hopefully, by chronicling his journey, many others will see that the 'light' is greater than the 'darkness.'"

—MIKE COFER, NFL KICKER (1987-95), SUPER BOWL CHAMPION (XXIII, XXIV), AND FIRST-TEAM ALL-PRO (1989)

"This story is one that must be told and Erik Kramer does just that, putting it all on the line as he did his life to share with us. No matter how bad it gets, there is always a way and a purpose to get through it!"

—CHRIS MYERS, FOX SPORTS EMMY AWARD-WINNING BROADCASTER
FOR THE NFL, MLB, AND NASCAR

"From his harrowing suicide attempt to his son's tragic death to the personal and familial relationships that shaped his life, Erik Kramer bravely provides an honest look at his rise to NFL stardom and his spiral to the depths of depression. *The Ultimate Comeback* is a compelling read for all."

—DAVE BIRKETT, *DETROIT FREE PRESS*, LIONS BEAT WRITER

"When you talk about a great teammate, a man of morals, a guy that can galvanize men, you think of Erik Kramer. I knew he would come through his trials and tribulations and become an example of resilience and reinventing oneself."

—LOMAS BROWN, NFL OFFENSIVE TACKLE (1985-2002), SEVEN-TIME PRO BOWLER,
SUPER BOWL CHAMPION (XXXVII), AND MEMBER OF THE COLLEGE FOOTBALL HALL OF FAME

"I've known Erik Kramer for over thirty years. His NFL career was incredible as he overcame unusual odds, but his football story is topped by his amazing life story. This book is a great inspiration to all, not just football fans. Erik is a winner on and off the football field."

—NORV TURNER, NCAA AND NFL COACH (1975-2019)
AND SUPER BOWL CHAMPION (XXVII, XXVIII)

"Erik Kramer was one of the greatest quarterbacks I had the honor to play alongside as a Detroit Lion. Even though, after leaving the NFL, he faced trials and tribulations beyond measure, he took that adversity and not only survived but remarkably THRIVED! Kramer played the game of football at a high level and is now winning the game of life!"

— MIKE UTLEY, DETROIT LIONS OFFENSIVE LINEMAN (1989-91) AND MEMBER OF THE COLLEGE FOOTBALL HALL OF FAME

"With striking candidness, Erik Kramer writes about football, fatherhood, failed relationships, and dances with death. There is tragedy in his words, but ultimately, this is a story about redemption."

— DAN POMPEI, NFL SENIOR WRITER FOR *THE ATHLETIC*

"As a player, Erik's work ethic, perseverance, and determination set him apart. After retiring from the NFL, we ran a passing camp together for high school quarterbacks and receivers. Throughout those years, I had no idea that he was dealing with all those issues. Erik is the embodiment of the ultimate comeback story. I know whoever reads this book will identify not only with the struggles Erik encountered but, more importantly, with the determination and perseverance it took for him to come out the other side. He is truly an extraordinary person with an amazing story."

— CURTIS CONWAY, NFL WIDE RECEIVER (1993-2004), NFL TV ANALYST, AND FOOTBALL STUDIO ANALYST FOR THE PAC-12 NETWORKS

"Erik Kramer was a starting NFL quarterback, and yet his most meaningful, impactful (and demanding) work has come after. Filled with bracing honesty and insight for all of us, *The Ultimate Comeback* tells the story of Erik's challenges, his recoveries, and his insistence to keep moving the chains."

—JON WERTHEIM, SENIOR WRITER FOR *SPORTS ILLUSTRATED* AND *60 MINUTES* CORRESPONDENT

"I had the privilege of coaching Erik for three seasons with the Chicago Bears. Because of his grit, determination, and unwavering confidence, in 1995, he had the best year of any Bears QB in team history. His 3,838 yards and 29 touchdowns are still team records. Erik overcame obstacles his entire career, but he maintained his belief in himself no matter what was thrown at him. He has gone through a lot and faced a tremendous amount of adversity but has battled through it because of his perseverance and determination. His story and this book will be an inspiration to many. Thanks, Erik."

—RON TURNER, BIG TEN COACH OF THE YEAR (2001) AND FORMER CHICAGO BEARS OFFENSIVE COORDINATOR

"As a former Pop Warner football teammate of Erik's turned best-selling author, I am extremely pissed he has written a book better than mine!"

—ADAM CAROLLA, COMEDIAN, ACTOR, AND HOST OF THE PODCAST *THE ADAM CAROLLA SHOW*

"Erik Kramer's second act is more remarkable than his first—and his first saw him post the greatest passing season in Bears history and lead the Lions to their only modern playoff win. He's clawed back from the edge, one daily miracle at a time."

—PATRICK FINLEY, *CHICAGO SUN-TIMES* BEARS REPORTER
AND COHOST OF THE PODCAST *HALAS INTRIGUE*

"Everyone who has played professional football endures hardship to some degree once the cheering stops. But I've never heard of *anyone* experiencing Erik Kramer's hell on earth. His story is chilling, yet how Erik got to the other side? That should inspire us all. He's a miracle."

—TYLER DUNNE, FOUNDER OF GO LONG

THE
ULTIMATE
COMEBACK

THE
ULTIMATE
COMEBACK

SURVIVING A SUICIDE ATTEMPT, CONQUERING DEPRESSION, AND LIVING WITH A PURPOSE

ERIK KRAMER

with WILLIAM CROYLE

Whitsett
Avenue
Publishing

The Ultimate Comeback: Surviving a Suicide Attempt, Conquering Depression, and Living with a Purpose

Whitsett Avenue Publishing
Agoura Hills, California
Email: whitsettavenuepublishing@gmail.com

Editor: Jennifer Huston Schaeffer of White Dog Editorial Services.
Cover photo: Karen Quincy Loberg.
Cover and interior design: Alan Dino Hebel & Ian Koviak, BookDesigners.com.

This book is a memoir that includes details of the author's personal experiences with and opinions about depression and suicide. While most of the dialogue comes from interviews with the speakers, other bits of dialogue have been re-created from the author's memory. This book is not intended as a substitute for medical advice from a qualified physician, licensed mental health professional, or other health-care providers. Information in this book is general and offered with no guarantees from the publisher or author. The publisher and author disclaim all liability in connection with the use of this book. Please contact the appropriate health-care providers for your condition if such services are needed.

If you are experiencing a mental health crisis or struggling with suicidal thoughts, you can contact the 988 Suicide & Crisis Lifeline by calling or texting 988 or using chat services at suicidepreventionlifeline.org to speak with a trained counselor.

Library of Congress Control Number: 2023917206

ISBN (paperback): 979-8-218-27927-1
ISBN (ebook): 979-8-218-27928-8

First Printing, 2023
Printed in the United States of America

To Griffen and Dillon—
You are the two eternal loves of my life.

CONTENTS

CHAPTER 1

DEAR DILLON, PART ONE

I hadn't set a date to kill myself. But after several intense weeks of planning, it struck me one Tuesday morning that the only task left was to pull the trigger.

I approached my imminent death like I would a football game: I meticulously studied an Internet "playbook" on suicide, plotted an effective strategy to execute it, and envisioned potential obstacles that might force me to call an audible. I even practiced firing my new pistol at the range. I was determined to win and hated to lose. Ironically, in this case, winning would mean losing everything. But depression didn't frame it that way. Instead, it assured me that this was my best option. Nothing else would be acceptable.

My process was emotionless, like a business transaction. The eight goodbye letters I'd written were the exceptions. Even then, when I penned a few sentences from the heart, I felt compelled to follow with a *but* to justify my exit. I wrote the letters alone one evening in the silence of my den, including one to my beloved younger son:

Dear Dillon,

I'm sorry for having to leave you. You're the only reason I have been pushing on as long as I have. My priority in life has always been to be a good father to you and Griffen. As I look back through the years, I put everything I had into it. But I also realize I was more flawed than I was probably ever aware.

I was born on November 6, 1964, and was an NFL quarterback for eleven years in the 1980s and '90s, an implausible feat given my lackluster résumé: I was second string on my high school varsity teams. No colleges recruited me. I wasn't good enough to start my first year at a junior college. Nineteen quarterbacks were among the 335 picks in the 1987 NFL draft—I wasn't one of them.

Yet, during the 1991 season, I helped lead the Detroit Lions to the league's third-best record and the franchise's first playoff win in thirty-four years. We were one victory shy of Super Bowl XXVI. With the Chicago Bears in 1995, I set single-season passing records that still stand as of this writing. My career lasted more than three times that of the average NFL player, and I played in more games than thirteen of those nineteen quarterbacks drafted in 1987. I even shared a TV screen with Al Bundy, starring as myself in an episode of the popular, long-running sitcom *Married . . . with Children*.

But behind the accomplishments and accolades, nobody knew the turmoil plaguing my brain.

Suicidal thoughts initially surfaced after I jumped to the Bears as a free agent in 1994. Though I bled silver and blue for four years in Detroit, the Lions didn't re-sign me. Meanwhile, Chicago pursued me like I was the next Joe Montana, offering a lucrative three-year deal. I took it but lost the starting job after four mediocre games and a separated shoulder. Depression, perceiving the crack in my spirit, slithered in and seized control.

I fought relentlessly to reclaim the starting role in 1995 and conquer depression for good. On the surface, it appeared that I'd succeeded. I started every game that season and finished with the league's fourth-highest quarterback rating behind Jim Harbaugh, Brett Favre, and Troy Aikman. I ranked ahead of superstars like Steve Young, Warren Moon, Dan Marino, and John Elway. One night out on the town, a friend and I entered a Chicago restaurant and heard someone shout, "Hey, EK! Over here!" It was basketball legend Michael Jordan waving me to his table. "Can you believe this?" I said in awe to my friend. "MJ called me EK!" I had every reason to believe that my darkest days were behind me.

But alas, it was all a ruse.

Depression plays dirty, by its own made-up rules, and it reemerged with a vengeance when spring practice began in 1996. The slightest self-doubts, failures, and criticisms promptly suffocated any achievements I had. Antidepressants were my saving grace, albeit a temporary one.

Looking back on myself as a kid, what stands out now, Dillon, is how much of a loner I was. And how uncomfortable I could be around peers and friends. Eventually, I was able to find some acceptance by accomplishing something through sports. But I was never able to feel 100 percent comfortable in my own skin. And now it feels like those feelings have just intensified and have no way of ever going away.

When I say I was a loner or uncomfortable, I wasn't necessarily unhappy. I was just an unassuming kid trying to find purpose and live virtuously. Even as a pro athlete, I stayed humble and laid low. I've never partied excessively or spent extravagantly. My indulgences were and still are being a dad, coaching football, golfing with my buddies, traveling, or reading a thought-provoking book.

The acceptance I discovered in sports fueled me to exert my utmost effort on the field, even when no one gave me a fighting chance. That's also where I found the motivation to live when I faced depression. The illness psychologically tormented me, much like the physical pain of having a strapping, three-hundred-pound defensive lineman slam me to the turf, play after play. Still, I always scraped my bruised and battered self off the ground and lined up again. My attitude, literally on the field and figuratively off, was that there was time on the clock, people relying on me, and a game to win. Each play signified new hope as I continually strived to be the best player, teammate, husband, father, son, brother, and friend.

So why did I eventually give up? Because on October 30, 2011, my older son, Griffen, died of a heroin overdose. Nine months later, my mother succumbed to uterine cancer. Weeks after her death, my father was diagnosed with terminal esophageal cancer. And since my divorce in 2012, I hadn't seen much of Dillon, who was living primarily with his mom.

My soul was shattered.

One by one, the people who mattered to me vanished. The most devastating loss was Griffen. He was an affable and intelligent eighteen-year-old with an indelible sense of humor. His interests were eclectic: He loved to play football—quarterback like his dad—and Albert Einstein and the late Bears' running back Walter Payton were his heroes. Italian tenor Andrea Bocelli and rapper Tupac Shakur were two of his favorite musicians.

After Griffen attended rehab before his senior year of high school, he appeared to come out a new person. But he couldn't entirely thwart his demons.

I tried to cope with the surge of grief in several ways, from psychologists to medication to treatment programs. Some helped, but none were steadfast solutions. Many believed I had chronic traumatic encephalopathy, or CTE, a brain disease associated with too many blows to the head and a common find in former NFL players. They may have been right, but CTE cannot be accurately diagnosed until the brain is analyzed postmortem. Even if I agreed with their assessment, I couldn't reverse the damage. Think how difficult it is for a healthy brain to digest so much human loss in such a short period of time. My broken one didn't stand a chance. I was done.

> Dillon, my mind no longer functions in a way that will allow me to keep living. Depression has come and gone in my life many times. And that is excruciating just by itself. But mentally, what has really intensified is self-doubt, slow thinking, a slipping memory, harshly judging myself, loneliness, not being able to maintain relationships, social anxiety, feeling too self-conscious to even speak, and then feeling dumb as a result, as well as many other negative thoughts. In terms of having a personal purpose to contribute or accomplish in life, I feel lost and empty.

That emptiness led me to Tuesday, August 18, 2015, when I realized that the only thing left was to end it.

The particulars of that morning and early afternoon are sketchy. I don't know if I ate, napped, read, cleaned the house, watched television, or called anyone. While some authors might fill that void with concocted stories, my life has been dramatic enough without the need to sensationalize. I'm a candid guy trying to help people struggling with depression. I want you to know the accurate details of my story as I know them to be true.

I recall waking up early, around seven or eight, at my home in Agoura Hills, California. It's a magnificent part of the country, about thirty-five miles west of Los Angeles and fifteen miles north of Malibu, along the northern edge of the Santa Monica Mountains. I showered, threw on a pair of shorts and a shirt, and went downstairs. That's when it hit me that everything was set. My financial affairs were in order. The gun was loaded with twelve rounds. And the letters to my family and friends were stacked neatly on my desk for someone to find.

> Dillon, you're an amazing, smart, loving, sensitive, kind person. You started out that way as a gorgeous baby and have never lost those characteristics. You've gone through so much at a young age. I know you're hurting over Griffen. And you've also been placed in the middle of a tough divorce for years. Maybe now with me gone, you won't feel stuck in the middle.

This was the first time my nerves were on edge. Not about the act of shooting myself—I was still in "business transaction" mode. I was uneasy about voluntarily leaving this life after fifty years. Relinquishing our human form and the space we've occupied on this earth to enter the unknown can be a scary prospect. But I'd made my decision. The depression prodded me to trust it and stay focused.

I retrieved the gun from my bedroom late in the afternoon, around four thirty or five, and stuffed it in a small overnight bag. I locked up the house, set the bag on the passenger seat of my car, and drove ten minutes east on the Ventura Freeway to the Good Nite Inn located in Calabasas. This was part of my plan. I wanted to commit the act close to home, but not *at* home. Dillon had a key, and I didn't want him to be the one to find my body.

After arriving at the hotel, the kind woman at the service desk assigned me a room on the second floor— the top floor.

You wouldn't give me the room if you knew what I was about to do, I thought to myself. *Or maybe you would, but then you'd call the police.*

Thoughts like that rattled around in my mind, but it wasn't a conscious attempt to deter myself. Quite the opposite, in fact. It was depression's subtle signal to maintain control of the situation. In other words, be cool and don't look suspicious.

I got to my room, flipped on the light, shut the door, slid the chain lock in place, and closed the curtains. The bed was to the left. To the right was a dresser and a television. The bathroom was straight ahead. *Perfect. A simple room for a short stay.*

I put the bag with the gun on the dresser, turned on the TV, and sat on the edge of the mattress. I stared mindlessly at the screen for about a minute or two. *What am I doing? This isn't some leisurely stay.* The depression was already impatient and kicking into high gear. *C'mon! Let's do this!*

Agitated by this onerous and familiar feeling, I stood up, turned off the TV, and decided it was time . . .

To eat.

Seriously. It was dinnertime, and I was famished.

By the way, please don't hesitate to laugh at things I say here or did then. Humor carries me through a lot nowadays. I've found it's an invaluable tool to combat depression. It also helps me share such a harrowing story. Like twelve rounds in a gun for a suicide attempt? Was I worried that I'd miss the first eleven times? Or the Good Nite Inn? Given why I was there, the irony of the name isn't lost on me.

With my stomach growling, I drove up the road to a small diner where my mom and I had once eaten, years earlier. I chose it on this particular day simply because it was familiar and nearby. I don't know what I ordered or what my server looked like. I don't even recall contemplating that this was my last supper. The mission at hand was to satisfy my hunger, and I accomplished it.

When I returned to the room around six o'clock, I refocused on my objective. I closed the door but left the chain lock off this time to make it easier for whoever came to my room first to get in. I carefully removed the gun from the bag, climbed onto the bed, and situated my back against the headboard. Besides practicing one day at the range, I hadn't shot a gun since I was about thirteen, and that was a pellet rifle while we were on vacation in the California desert. Granted, these were two different types of guns, but this shot would be point-blank. It couldn't be any simpler, right?

I repeatedly swapped the gun for my phone for roughly the next two hours. I'd hold the gun. Stare at it. Set it down. Pick up my phone. Scroll through it. Set it down. Pick up the gun. Was I stalling? Maybe. But I was more anxious about the specifics of my plan. Did I cover *everything*? The bills? The letters? My will? When I finally convinced myself that I had, I set down the gun one last time, grabbed my phone, and fired off several text messages.

One was to my younger sister, Kelley, my lone sibling. She lived four hours away in Las Vegas. I explained, in short, that it was time for me to go. I told her I loved her and to hug her two teenage boys, whom I adored, for me. Another text was to my old high school friend, Chris Germann.

"Hey, buddy," I texted him. "When 911 is called, I'm at the Good Nite Inn in Calabasas." I gave him my room number and ended with, "Please take care of Dillon for me."

Chris and I hadn't spoken to each other in a while, but, in retrospect, reaching out to him made sense for two reasons. One was that we'd reconnected nearly four years earlier when Griffen had died, so he knew the agony I'd suffered. The other was that he was an officer with the LA County Sheriff's Department, which had jurisdiction over Calabasas, where I was. Was this a cry for help? Did I want someone to stop me?

But, unbeknownst to me at the time, Chris was in New Orleans, moving his son into his new place for college, so he didn't see my message right away. When he did read it, several minutes after I sent it, his heart sank. By then, Chris had been a cop for thirty years, so he knew exactly what I was doing. And because I gave him my location, he had no doubt that it was a cry for help.

I would later find out that Kelley received my text immediately and called, but I didn't answer. She then desperately tried to contact numerous people, including my good friend Eric Hipple, who was also a former quarterback for the Lions. An expert on depression, Eric had worked with me that summer to beat the disease. But Eric was at the movies that night, so his phone was muted after a long day of suicide prevention work at a US Navy base in Seattle.

After sending those texts, it was approaching eight o'clock. I dropped the phone on the bed and picked up the gun.

This is it.

I held the weapon tightly with my right hand, wrapping my left hand around the right one for maximum support. With my right index finger on the trigger, I took a long, deep breath and thought about Dillon.

I loved my son so much that it hurt. He was incredibly bright, athletic, and on his way to earning a college baseball scholarship. By the age of seventeen, he'd been through tremendous heartbreak with his brother's death and his parents' divorce. He would later ask me why I wanted to end my life if I loved him so much. It's a fair question with a complex answer that I continue to navigate with him today. It also might help others better understand depression, which is why I challenged myself to write my story. The short answer is that my brain was profoundly sick. It's not an excuse; it was my condition. As my close friend Anna Dergan has said, no father in his right mind who loves his children as much as I do would ever think that leaving them is a solution for anything. All I wanted was to breathe again, and I was genuinely convinced that the only way I could was to take my last breath. Now, I cannot think of anything more illogical.

Dillon, I love you with all that I have ever had and all that I have left. You have so much goodness inside you. I believe you will still find your passion and have a good life. I can't get around feeling like a complete failure and a coward for not trying to keep living on your behalf. And I couldn't blame you if you hate me in the end. Just know I did the best I could for as long as I could.

With both hands clenching the gun, I pressed the cold barrel under my chin and moved it around until it settled firmly into the flesh of my lower jaw. Then I took one more deep breath, closed my eyes, and pulled the trigger.

CHAPTER 2

THE PECULIAR MARRIAGE
OF EILEEN AND KARL

I believe the essence of a person's character and behavior—their strengths, shortcomings, and everything in between—can often be traced to the environments in which they were raised. I'm no exception.

To make sense of that tragic night in the hotel room and beyond, you should know about my life prior. Let me guide you on a bizarre and fascinating journey that begins with my eccentric parents, Eileen and Karl Kramer. They were good people at their cores but not so much to each other. The result was a joyless, twenty-year-long marriage that created a turbulent climate for Kelley and me.

Dad was a couple years older than Mom. They both attended Van Nuys High School, which is about ten miles northwest of Hollywood, but they didn't meet until after Mom graduated. They dated briefly before deciding on a whim to run away and get married. My Aunt Patrice (Mom's sister) told me that their father tried to quell their urgency by offering to throw an elegant affair with family and friends, but the adventure of eloping was too

Mom and Dad during one of their happier moments in their younger years.
(Photo courtesy: Erik Kramer)

enticing. They drove to Las Vegas, found a cheap walk-in wedding chapel, and returned to Southern California a couple days later as newlyweds.

And the honeymoon was over forever.

I used to wonder when and why Mom and Dad's love soured, but I've concluded that they probably never truly loved one another. At the same time, they didn't hate each other—that would've required a commitment, and neither was willing to put that much effort into the relationship. There was a considerable lack of respect between them that amplified over time. No drugs. No alcohol. Just a glut of antipathy.

Their absence of affection for each other didn't preclude them from loving Kelley and me, but they struggled to show it. I grew up with anxiety, fear of failure, and little confidence. I was afraid of not being good enough at anything. If there was one positive from that, it was the strong work ethic I developed in my quest to always be better. But it wasn't the healthiest way to parent a shy kid simply looking for acceptance from his mom and dad. About the only time they showed their love, or knew how to, was when it came to sports. The best word to describe my relationship with them back then is *incomplete*.

My mother was tough, self-driven, disciplined, organized, and focused. Those qualities generally make for a good athlete, and she was phenomenal. She played or coached basketball, softball, soccer, track, golf, and tennis. As a kid, she was the perennial tetherball champion on the school playground. At thirty—with a husband, two children, and a full-time job as an office manager—she ran track as a sprinter and played basketball at California State University, Northridge. She wasn't just a student-athlete; she was a student-wife-mother-working-athlete and an inspiration to her teenage teammates. Even in her middle-aged years, she dashed out of the house every morning at five o'clock to play racquetball before work.

After earning her degree in physical education, she wanted to teach. However, she never left her job as an office manager because she was too loyal to her boss to pursue her own dreams.

Mom's competitiveness was just as extreme at home. Challenge her, and it was game on. Horseshoes, badminton, table tennis, a race to the kitchen, whatever. She was also big into cards. When she and Patrice played canasta,

Patrice wasn't allowed to quit until Mom was satisfied with the results. In slapjack, if I slapped a jack a split second before Mom did, she'd smack my knuckles with enough sting to make me think twice about beating her again. When she played "mercy" with Griffen and Dillon—a game in which you bend a person's wrists backward until they give up—she showed them none. They'd end up dropping to their knees, writhing in pain. The boys were maybe ten and five years old at the time, but that didn't matter. She loved her grandsons, but her opponents' ages, skill levels, and relationship to her were irrelevant when it came to competition. Winning was all that mattered.

Mom and Griffen playing "mercy." *(Photo courtesy: Erik Kramer)*

Given our shared athleticism, one would expect that I had a close relationship with my mom while I was growing up. I wish it were true.

Mom had an aversion toward me, and I felt that it was for one weird reason: I shared my dad's genes and reminded her of him. She habitually spoke to me in irritated and condescending tones. She'd get angry if she found a couch pillow out of place when she got home from work. If I popped open a can of soda, she'd scream at me for wasting a drink "meant for guests." She frequently embarrassed me in front of my friends, yelling at me and dragging me home for not doing a minor chore. Even though I was quiet and easygoing, I was often a thorn in her side just for existing. Yes, there were many good times. She took Kelley and me on weekend trips (usually without Dad), played ball with us, and enjoyed watching our games. But she lacked a natural maternal component that my friends' moms seemed to have.

Mom was the oldest of five children that included Patrice, Martha, Kim, and Kirk. But Martha died as a toddler when she fell out of a car window. After that incident, their father became overly strict. As products of our past, I'm sure my mom was deeply affected by hers, which could explain her struggle to rear her own children. Later, when she sensed my depression in the mid-1990s, Mom revealed her unconditional love for me, and our relationship grew from there, but it was a long road for both of us.

And then there was my dad. While I also have fond memories of him, he was the quintessential example of a father living vicariously through his son. He knew no boundaries and meddled in my life well into my adulthood—mainly to satisfy his ego and occasionally for personal gain.

My dad was a stubborn man who refused to change. In fairness, he had an unstable childhood too—one that was even worse than my mom's. His mother abandoned the family when he was young, and his father sent him to rural Oklahoma to live with an aunt. I've heard that kids raised in stressful environments sometimes become "addicted to chaos" or "wired for drama" as they age. That was my dad. He worked as a salesman, peddling products such as sprinkler systems, office supplies, and furniture. Heck, given his ability to sweet-talk his way into or out of anything, he probably could've sold water to a fish. But underneath it all, he was an odd character who couldn't establish or maintain healthy relationships, even with those who graciously helped him. For those reasons, he struggled to hold a job or anyone's trust.

His admirable qualities as a father revolved around coaching Kelley and me. Before our baseball or softball games, he'd often mow the grass at the fields, which the city didn't maintain to his standards. He loved teaching and had terrific patience with his players—even those less skilled—and relished the challenge to make them better. Comedian and award-winning podcast host Adam Carolla was one of my Pop Warner youth football teammates. He recently told me that after riding the bench most of the first year my dad coached him, Dad was thrilled to see Adam sign up again the following fall. It meant so much to Adam that Dad didn't give up on him. Adam continued playing football through high school on both sides of the ball and earned All-League honors his senior year. It was a rare and pleasing story about my father, who didn't make it easy for anyone to love him.

Dad, Kelley, and me.
(Photo courtesy: Erik Kramer)

Like my mom, my dad was about winning and devised unconventional ways to give his teams the best chance against any opponent. For example, one Saturday when I was ten, our basketball team played the top team in the league. This team had such a high-powered offense that thirty-point blowouts were the norm. Dad countered by ordering us into a four-corners offense for the entire game. The premise was simple: spread out across the floor and pass the ball until they come to guard us. When they do, work the ball inside for a basket. When they don't, let the clock tick away. In the old days, this was called "stall ball," a boring yet legal way to slow down the other team. Dad refused to budge as the other team's parents vocally complained throughout the game. We won, 12–10, and Dad made no apologies.

Athletics, unfortunately, also brought out the worst in him. When I was twelve and in a baseball all-star tournament, we were in the losers' bracket and had to win twice against the top team from the winners' bracket. As our best pitcher, I was slated to throw the first game. Dad, who wasn't our coach, thought I should pitch the second game instead. We were taking pregame infield practice when Dad called me over to the fence.

"Tell your coach you need to pitch the second game, not the first," he insisted.

"Why?"

"Because if you win the first game, there's nobody good enough to pitch the second one. Go tell him now."

"No!" I protested. "I'm not telling my coach what to do!"

"You tell him right now!" Dad ordered, gritting his teeth and waving his finger at me. Our argument escalated into a humiliating scene in front of my teammates and their parents. I threw down my glove, sprinted to an empty field across the way, and sobbed alone in the dugout. My outburst caused my coach to scratch me from the lineup altogether. There would be no second game for anyone.

In a later incident, when I was playing football and baseball for a local junior college, I elected to quit baseball to focus on football. When I told Dad, he released his rage by punching his fist through our living room wall. I didn't expect such an overreaction, though maybe I should have. To Dad, it was one less sport I would have a chance to play professionally. This is how passionate he was about me achieving his dream.

In hindsight, my parents' happiest times together were when other people were around. Mom and Dad loved throwing neighborhood parties, playing doubles tennis, co-coaching teams, and playing cards with friends. But when they had no external buffers to distract them from each other, they functioned with little joy. When I was in high school, Mom confided in me that she wanted a divorce, but she said Dad had threatened suicide when she'd broached the subject. She didn't think he was serious, but she wasn't certain, so she stuck it out for Kelley and me until she was sure he was no longer a threat to himself.

My mom and dad had several objectionable flaws and quirks, which were largely consequences of their unconventional upbringings. But I still loved them. Despite their minimal knowledge of how to be good parents and role models, I came to realize that they did their best with what they had. Growing up in the Kramer household also taught me that we can craft our guiding principles not only by following the good examples of those around us but also by choosing not to emulate the bad ones. I can't claim that I've been the perfect son, brother, husband, or father. Sometimes I've repeated my parents' mistakes. But many of my better judgments have resulted from what I've learned *not* to do from them. Unfortunately, in some cases, it took me years to acquire that wisdom.

CHAPTER 3

ALWAYS THE NEW KID

Only my dad acknowledged my pro potential, and I'm not sure he *saw* it as much as he *wanted* it.

I was a natural in football, baseball, and basketball as early as elementary school. Basketball was my best sport, but I had the most fun playing the other two. I wasn't flashy, just a decent athlete who hustled and had an innate drive to be better. Dad and I never discussed my talent or my future. I just kept my head down and played while he served as my micromanager. And although I don't think he cared which sport I excelled in, football was always the catalyst for his decisions.

My Pop Warner football days. *(Photos courtesy: Erik Kramer)*

We lived in Canoga Park in the San Fernando Valley region of Los Angeles. I was a geek in high school—slender, six feet tall, and 165 pounds, with braces and bushy brown hair. Starting my freshman year, in 1978, I should've attended Canoga Park High School, but, instead, Dad sent me about thirty minutes east to the now-defunct Valley Christian School in Van Nuys. We weren't religious, but he knew the football coach and thought it would be an ideal fit for me.

It wasn't.

The school was so small that we played in a league of eight-man teams. I remember almost nothing about that season or the school, and Dad wasn't impressed either. After one semester, he transferred me to St. Genevieve in Panorama City, a Catholic institution about ten minutes north of Valley Christian.

I liked St. Genevieve—the kids and the classes—but it proved fruitless for Dad's goals. I only played three games as the junior varsity quarterback during my sophomore year before breaking my collarbone. As a junior, I served as the backup varsity quarterback. My lone good memory of that season is coming in for mop-up duty in the fourth quarter of a game we were losing by about four touchdowns. Our coach, Lindon Crow, was a three-time NFL Pro Bowl defensive back in the 1950s and '60s for the Chicago Cardinals, New York Giants, and Los Angeles Rams. In 1956, while with the Cardinals, he led the NFL with eleven interceptions. With the Giants, he intercepted future Hall of Famer Johnny Unitas in the

One of the few games I played at St. Genevieve. *(Photo courtesy: Erik Kramer)*

1958 NFL championship game, which has been dubbed "The Greatest Game Ever Played."

On my first play, Coach Crow called for a pass. He instructed one receiver to go to the right corner of the end zone and another to head toward the goalpost.

"No matter what, Kramer, do *not* throw it to the post receiver," he commanded. "That safety is good and will intercept it."

So I rolled out, looked downfield, and heaved the ball toward the post receiver. I didn't intend to defy Coach Crow; I just thought the receiver was open enough for me to hit him. As the ball sailed through the air and descended toward the goal line, it slipped right through the safety's hands and into my receiver's arms for a touchdown. Nine times out of ten, that safety would've picked it off. I couldn't have been luckier.

"Kramer!" Coach Crow barked as I jogged to the sidelines triumphantly. "What are you doing? You threw the ball right where I told you not to! He should've intercepted that!"

But he didn't. And we scored. Why are you yelling at me? The only wise decision I made that night was to keep those thoughts in my head.

We weren't very good that season, and the JV quarterback moving up to varsity during my senior year showed a lot of promise. Expecting that I'd be beat out for the starting slot, Dad transferred me again, this time to John Burroughs High School in Burbank.

Dad's behavior probably seemed random to the average spectator, but there was a method to his madness. He tracked the talent at my school, took handwritten notes on players he'd scouted at other schools, and thought he knew exactly how I would or wouldn't fit into a team's system. It was an obsession. He overcoached and overparented, but he had a vision for me and was determined to see it through. Had I spent four steady years at Canoga Park with my neighborhood friends, I'm confident that I would've thrived athletically, academically, and socially. Instead, I continually started from scratch and was always "the new kid." I didn't resist because it wasn't my personality. Dad told me where I would go next and why, selling it to me as any good salesman would. I never liked the idea, but I didn't argue or dwell on it. I simply adapted to each new school and pushed forward.

My biggest adjustment—one beyond my wildest imagination but not Dad's, of course—came while I was at Burroughs. The school, which was about an hour east of us, was renowned for its gridiron success. Most of the students grew up in the community, and all were required to live in the district so that outsiders like me wouldn't attend purely for sports. But Dad found a way to skirt the rule.

"Erik, you're going to live with Jantz and his dad at their apartment in Burbank," he sprung on me one day the summer before my senior year.

"I'm what? Who?"

Jantz was an old friend I hadn't seen since middle school football. Back then, my dad and Jantz's dad, Darryl, coached our team together for a year. By this time, Jantz and Darryl were living in an apartment in Burbank, and Jantz was going to be playing football for Burroughs. When Dad found out, he reconnected with Darryl and convinced him to let me crash with them and pledged to pay them rent. This wasn't an unusual ploy in football-rich Southern California; in other words, my dad wasn't the only parent doing it. I knew that didn't make it okay, but it was justifiable in Dad's book.

Living in an apartment with another family was one of the strangest times of my young life. I slept on the floor in the living room. Darryl worked long hours but cooked enough food each morning for Jantz and me to get by after school and into the evening. Dad stuck his head in once or twice a week and usually took me home for the weekends. I'm sure he thought that was enough to fulfill his obligation as a good father. Mom never said a word about the situation. Had she interfered, a worthless argument with Dad, no doubt, would've ensued. I never was comfortable living with Darryl and Jantz. They didn't make me feel unwelcome, but I felt like I was infringing on them when I had my own family.

In addition to the living arrangements, as I reminisce about that time, it brings back a couple unpleasant memories. One is that I didn't fit in at Burroughs. Making new friends is always hard, especially when you're starting your senior year at a new high school. Everyone already had their friends and didn't necessarily want more. Every day at lunchtime, I ate a peanut butter and jelly sandwich in the coach's office by myself while watching game film. It allowed me to be reclusive while also looking dedicated to my coaches. A classmate once asked me why I didn't eat in the cafeteria with everyone else. I had no answer for her. I was just most comfortable alone.

The other troublesome reminder of this time is that I'm convinced my dad never paid Darryl for housing me. I don't have any actual proof, but I never saw Dad give him a dime. It also would've been in line with my dad's character to weasel his way into getting what he wanted but not follow through on his end of the bargain. Darryl, being the nice guy he was, never held it against me. I tried to repay the debt a few years later, in 1987, when Darryl was diagnosed with a terminal illness. I was only twenty-three at the time and had a relatively small one-year contract with the Atlanta Falcons during my first season in the NFL. But I was sad about Darryl's situation and wanted to help by giving some money to his family. I also felt a moral obligation given Darryl's generosity toward me and my dad's lack of commitment to him.

I can honestly say that I wouldn't have made it to the NFL without my dad. I just wish he would've taken a more ethical and empathetic approach in how he dealt with people—especially with Darryl, who was so good to us.

Despite my awkward time at Burroughs, my senior football season was fun, even though I played defense. We had another senior quarterback who grew up in Burbank and was clearly better than me. This relevant nugget of information had somehow slipped past Dad's scouting report. Nevertheless, our coach held an open competition between us. After equal playing time in the first four games, which resulted in two wins and two losses, our coach kept the other guy at quarterback and moved me to free safety. Both were genius moves. We didn't lose another game until the league championship, and I earned all-league second-team honors on defense.

Toward the end of the season, our defensive backs coach asked me if I wanted to play at a small college after graduation. He thought I was good enough and was willing to call schools on my behalf.

"Thanks, Coach," I said, "but I don't think so."

I enjoyed playing safety—it was nice to hit someone rather than be hit—but the only position I wanted to play in college was quarterback. However, it's difficult to be recruited or sell yourself as a quarterback when you've hardly played it since middle school. I figured my senior year of high school would be my last in football, and I was willing to accept that.

But Dad wasn't.

CHAPTER 4

"IT'S A LOSER SCHOOL"

On a blistering afternoon in the summer of 1983, we were laboring through conditioning drills at Los Angeles Pierce College when a teammate nudged me.

"Hey, isn't that your dad by the trees?" he asked, nodding toward a grove overlooking the field. When the distant figure came into focus, I sighed with shame. I'd asked Dad to stop sitting in the bleachers during our practices. It was embarrassing, and none of the other parents did it. Seemingly respecting my wishes, he'd migrated a few hundred feet away where he thought the trees would camouflage him. I didn't say anything after practice. I simply didn't want to expend any more energy nagging him about his idiosyncrasies. I also felt indebted to him since he was why I'd gotten a shot at Pierce.

During the spring of my senior year at Burroughs, Dad had finagled his way into the office of Pierce's head coach, Jim Fenwick. After I'd played safety for an entire season, Dad probably realized that if I had a chance to play quarterback anywhere collegiately, it would be at Pierce—a local junior college. He convinced Coach Fenwick to let me practice with the team each day after school, which allowed the staff to assess my talent before I actually enrolled. The irony is that when I was growing up, whenever someone mentioned Pierce, Dad would scoff, "It's a loser school!" He was confident that his son would lead a powerhouse like USC or UCLA to the Rose Bowl one day. However, Dad was also a fan of the underdog, which may explain his abiding faith in me and newfound love for Pierce.

I gray-shirted my first year in the fall of 1982. That meant I attended classes and the team was committed to me, but I couldn't play or practice that season. However, I did play baseball in the spring of 1983—a little third base and shortstop. I didn't see the field much or do too well when I did because I hadn't picked up a bat or ball since the previous spring season at Burroughs. But I still enjoyed the game.

That summer, when preseason football practices started, I competed for the starting job with a quarterback who was a year older than me—and I lost. Coming in second was nothing new, and I generally handled it well, but this time, Coach Fenwick's decision infuriated me. I'd done everything he and my dad had asked of me: I'd practiced with the team while in high school, sat out my first year, and worked out in the off-season when I wasn't on a baseball diamond. But apparently, none of that mattered.

I visibly carried that negative attitude through the early part of the regular season. I sulked on the sidelines and silently griped during games rather than helping our quarterback and coaches strategize. When I lost the starting job at Burroughs, they moved me to defense. At Pierce, they sat me on the bench.

Around midseason, with coaches and teammates rightfully ignoring my petulance, I had an epiphany to detach myself from the situation and examine my behavior from the outside looking in. This enabled me to recognize and concede how selfish I was being. I knew I had a decision to make: quit the team or grow up.

I opted for the latter.

What jarred some sense into me was how poorly I'd played when Coach Fenwick had sent me in one game late in the fourth quarter. I was disgraceful with missed reads and horrible throws. I could sense that my teammates had no confidence in me in the huddle. I knew my attitude was bad, but now I could see its toxicity affecting the team. I realized then how presumptuous I'd been to expect the coaches to hand me the quarterback job over an upperclassman. And what did I think pouting would do? This wasn't youth football. We were adults. I could be part of something bigger than me or not.

I've since learned through a coaching course I took that there are two types of athletes—ego-driven and task-driven. I was the poster child for both at Pierce. The ego-driven athlete is concerned about himself. He cares about whether *he* wins or loses. He sets out to destroy everything and everyone in his path for his benefit, and if he fails, he quits. The task-driven athlete is unfettered by personal stats. He finds pleasure in making those around him better, and his mission is the team's mission.

I was ego-driven when I lost the starting job. I psychologically quit on my coaches, teammates, and myself. While the game was at one end of the field, I chose to stand isolated at the other end. As a result, when the coach sent me into a game, my performance was pathetic. When I transitioned to a task-driven approach, I worked hard at practice, paid attention in film sessions, and helped the starting quarterback during games. From that point forward, I was team-focused. I didn't worry about getting into a game but knew I would succeed when I did.

I used to wonder if my ego-driven self stemmed from witnessing my father's behavior for so long. He was always raving about my talent to coaches as if I were the next Roger Staubach or Terry Bradshaw. Now I'm *sure* Dad's actions played a role in my motives. My dad was an ego-driven person. His life was great as long as people helped him get what he wanted. But as soon as things went south, he blamed everyone but himself. That was me at Pierce; however, I realized my dad was no excuse for my conduct. No matter the origin of my temperament, it was entirely up to me to change who I'd become. Fortunately, I broke that cycle and became a task-driven person. That rebirth was a monumental stepping stone to everything good in my football career.

In the spring of 1984, I quit baseball after a few games to focus on football, which, as noted earlier, prompted Dad to punch his fist through the wall. In the fall—my third year as a student at Pierce and second year of playing football—I earned the starting quarterback job and led our team to an undefeated season. We were ranked number one in the country and played in the Potato Bowl for the national championship. How's that for a task-driven attitude adjustment? We lost in the Potato Bowl to Taft College, but after several years of trying to prove that I could play quarterback at a high-caliber level and be a team leader, I'd finally done it—and people had noticed.

That's me about to take a snap for Pierce.
(Photo courtesy: Erik Kramer)

Toward the end of that season, with two years of college football eligibility left, I was inundated with letters from respectable Division I schools like Illinois, Pitt, Miami of Ohio, San Jose State, and North Carolina State. Coaches visited me and invited me to explore their campuses. Then scholarship offers rolled in. I took it all in stride and, surprisingly, so did Dad. He threw in his two cents now and then, but he pretty much retreated to the background as I weighed my options. He knew that no matter which school I picked, I would be a Division I quarterback. In his mind, I'm sure that alone was vindication for his perpetual interference in my life.

I narrowed my choices to Illinois, Pitt, and North Carolina State. I visited Illinois and Pitt, but they were set at quarterback for the 1985 season and wanted me for the following year. NC State, however, had no established quarterback. When I flew to the school for an official visit, the coaches assured me that I would compete equally in practice with two other junior college recruits—both coincidentally from California—for the starting quarterback position.

The challenge intrigued me, so I was all in.

In January 1985, weeks after the Potato Bowl, I said goodbye to my family and headed twenty-five hundred miles east to my new home. Within a few short years, thanks to a ton of hard work, good luck, and an exceedingly intrusive father, I'd gone from being an unrecruited high school defensive back to earning the starting quarterback job for the North Carolina State Wolfpack in the Atlantic Coast Conference.

CHAPTER 5

A NEW LIFE

Perhaps it goes without saying, but Raleigh, North Carolina, was a bit of a culture shock for this Southern Californian who'd rarely left the comfort of his home state. It was eight degrees when I deplaned in shorts, a T-shirt, and flip-flops. One day when I trudged to class through two inches of snow, it might as well have been a foot. Many natives had their own colloquialisms and such thick southern accents that I wondered if I needed an interpreter. And KKK marches, some at the state capitol just a few miles from campus, were not uncommon.

Starting over in an unfamiliar setting wasn't new to me, but NC State was a different ball game. I was truly on my own and had to mature quickly, especially in the classroom. I was always a good student, but my transience in high school made it difficult to reach my potential. At NC State, I was excited to become educated, self-sufficient, and prepared for life after football. Maybe too excited because I made the mistake of picking zoology as a major, which lasted just one semester. I wanted to work with animals, but the science was much too complicated for my liking. In the fall, I switched my major to speech communication. Perhaps it was an odd choice for an introvert, but I was intrigued by the idea of challenging myself socially.

A few months after I settled in, my mom called me one night to say she and my dad had separated and filed for divorce. I told her I was sorry, but the words were hollow because I was thinking to myself, *What took you so long?* Needless to say, I was relieved, as I'm sure she and Dad were. It was long overdue.

The best explanation I found for my parents' marriage was in a book by Dr. Harville Hendrix titled *Getting the Love You Want.* I gleaned from it that we often think we're attracted to people who display the positive qualities we seek in a companion. However, we are actually enticed by their negative qualities because that allows us to keep our undesirable traits. That may be the reason why many couples don't get along. Why else would my parents tolerate each other for as long as they did? They were seldom happy. Their marriage looked nothing like what my friends' parents had or what I saw on wholesome television shows such as *Happy Days* or *The Waltons.* My mom and dad lived separate lives, pitted themselves against each other, and put their individual desires first. And they clung to those egocentric attitudes right through their divorce proceedings. Mom said Dad agreed to divorce this time because he saw it as an opportunity for himself, which she saw as an opportunity for herself. She told me she was buying Dad's half of the house and would continue to live there.

"And your father and Kelley will be moving to North Carolina to be closer to you so they can watch you play," Mom said matter-of-factly.

What?

I couldn't believe it. The prospect of Dad being so close after I'd finally put some space between us was exasperating. But what could I do? And it was even worse for Kelley.

Kelley and I had a good relationship as kids, despite our significant age difference. I was six and a half when she was born. To put this into context, I was in high school when she was in third grade. Kelley was an outstanding athlete, the best among her peers. Softball, basketball, soccer—she excelled at everything. But that and everything else good in her life was uprooted when she was forced to move to North Carolina just as she hit her formative teen years. She had to leave her school, friends, teammates, coaches, and the only home she'd ever known—not to mention our mother, who didn't fight to keep her. That's something I cannot explain, but I know it must've hurt Kelley. At least I had a choice to move and a purpose for going. Kelley had neither. She was stuck under the authority of a childish parent who couldn't hold a job and was more attentive to his son's football exploits than raising his daughter. And with a daily schedule full of classes and practices, I couldn't do much to help her. She likely had little guidance or supervision, which wasn't fair to her.

Dad found sales jobs in North Carolina, but they were all short-lived. He loved earning hefty commissions with one-time sales but was averse to the daily grind of making a living with an hourly or salaried job, which he especially needed without Mom's support. He would make a nice commission, spend it all, then struggle to earn the next one. He would bounce from job to job, often dropping my name to further his own agenda. *Hey, I'm Karl Kramer. You know, my son, Erik, is the quarterback at NC State.* When I was young, Dad once told me that he was not cut out for the business world, but I think he meant he wasn't cut out for the working world.

I appreciated Dad watching me play at NC State, but our strained relationship declined further because of his erratic behavior. A couple weeks into my first season with the Wolfpack, he wandered down to the field after a game to talk with my coaches. He even popped into their offices once "to chat." I had to tell him explicitly to stop. It was vexing enough in high school and at Pierce. But at a Division I college? He assumed no boundaries existed if I didn't clearly define them. Even when I did, I think he thought the lines I drew were dotted, leaving a way for him to cross them.

Regardless of Dad's ways, I fixated on succeeding at NC State and had notable stats during my junior year, my first season there. I led the ACC in pass attempts, completions, passing yards, and passing touchdowns. The downside was that we finished 3–8, including an upset loss at home to Furman University, a Division 1–AA team. But, as I learned throughout high school and junior college, sometimes you have to plow through adversity to reach your destination. At the end of the season, NC State hired Furman's head coach, Dick Sheridan, to guide the team my senior year—and we totally reversed course. We finished 8-3-1 in 1986, came in second place in the ACC, beat three Top 20 teams, were ranked as high as fifteenth in the country, and earned a berth in the Peach Bowl. My stats weren't as solid as the previous season, but my leadership in our turnaround was recognized when I was named the ACC Player of the Year. I was the first Wolfpack quarterback to achieve the honor since Roman Gabriel in 1961 and the last until Philip Rivers in 2003.

I know my dad was proud of my accomplishments. I didn't ask for his input, and all he said after victories—or that I would give him time to say—was "Good game!" or "Congratulations!" He probably bragged plenty to anyone who would listen, especially if he thought it would net him something. I'm thrilled that he got to watch me play quarterback at a high level after all the effort he put into grooming me, but I think keeping a healthy distance from him during the season was critical to my success. Even the dotted-line boundaries were better than none at all.

My overall experience at NC State was influential to my growth as a person and continues to resonate with me today. I love Raleigh and return when I can. Many of my Wolfpack teammates are still my friends, and Coach Sheridan, who sadly passed away in July 2023, was one of the best I ever played for. Accepting the university's scholarship offer was the start of a new life for me, something I desperately needed.

It took some adjusting, but I eventually settled in at NC State.

(Photo courtesy: NC State University, Library Special Collections)

However, there was one drawback that many of us encounter when starting anew: loneliness. Football, classes, and hanging out with my teammates occupied vast chunks of my time, but I was still homesick. One would think the quarterback of a major college program could easily immerse himself into his new surroundings, especially socially and with women, but I was too reticent. To fill that void, I asked Marshawn, my girlfriend back home in California, to join me around the same time that my parents split.

Marshawn and I had dated on and off during my senior year at John Burroughs High School and while I was at Pierce. In the summer of 1985, after my first semester at NC State, I asked her to move to North Carolina. She wasn't in school and was working as a waitress in California, a job that she could find in Raleigh if she wanted, and she eventually would. We lived together for nearly two years before getting married in 1987, during spring break of my senior year. The wedding was a lovely ceremony that took place among family and friends in the historic chapel at Oxford College, which is part of Emory University in Atlanta, where her father worked. By all accounts, it was a marriage made in heaven. But in retrospect, we were too young, too immature, and too distant in our personal goals. A few months after we tied the knot, I wanted to get out the scissors and cut myself loose. By December of that same year, I asked for a divorce.

CHAPTER 6

THE ONLY WOMAN
WHO DIDN'T SCARE ME

Growing up, girls and women intimidated me. My dad once told me never to trust them. I mistakenly believed him because I was young and impressionable and wasn't always treated well by my mom. But I knew he was wrong when I met Marshawn.

Marshawn was Jantz's cousin. We met when she came over to the apartment one day to visit Darryl and Jantz, and we were instantly enamored with one another. She was a year and a half older than me, a free spirit, and the only woman I'd ever known who didn't scare me. There was no judgment—no criticism. We felt safe together and confided in each other through conversations I couldn't have had with anyone else. But as romantic and magical as that may sound, it wasn't meant to be.

Ultimately, Marshawn and I were both to blame for the continual failures of our relationship. Looking back, I think a couple of underlying factors heavily contributed to our downfall. One was our mutually unsettling pasts. You know mine. I had an immature father who wasn't much of a role model and a domineering mother who made me feel inadequate. It isn't my place to discuss the details of Marshawn's upbringing, but generally speaking, I think she also lacked guidance and faced many challenges through no fault of her own. As a result, she struggled to find direction in her life. In that sense, I saw my father in her, and some psychiatrists may say that's what attracted me to her. I didn't admire my dad, but for better or worse, he and my mom were my two primary influences growing up. Finding a partner with his attributes was subconsciously more desirable than someone with my mom's, which I consciously avoided because of the way she treated me.

The other factor was that in my early twenties, my life abruptly transformed in a major way. When Marshawn and I first met and dated in those early years, we were both lost souls on equal ground who found comfort in each other and rarely in anything or anyone else. But then, unexpectedly, schools nationwide began offering me scholarships, and their coaches were eager to mentor me. All at once, I had the opportunity to escape the chaos of home and pursue a degree from a major university while playing football. And although going pro was not on my radar then, it eventually would be.

In short, I'd found purpose and on a much higher level than anything I'd ever experienced. Or maybe it would be more accurate to say that purpose found me. Either way, my life was suddenly on a new and exciting path. What attracted Marshawn and me to each other at the outset faded as opportunities came my way, and the emotional distance between us expanded.

In the fall of 1987, about eight months after we had wed, Marshawn and I separated. When nothing had improved in the couple of months after that, I told her around Christmas that I wanted a divorce. When she informed her father, he asked to speak with me. I'd always respected him and was willing to listen.

"Erik, I'm not going to try to talk you out of it," he said. "But it seems to me that you and Marshawn have had a decent history together, and you haven't been married long. You should think about this more."

I understood his assessment. On paper and from an outsider's perspective, ten months of marriage didn't seem like much effort. I also did some soul-searching and realized that I'd spent most of my young life overcoming adversity, whether it involved my parents, school, or football. Marriage was more substantial than any of those, so I figured, why not keep fighting to make it work? With that, I decided to give the marriage another chance. And I continued to have that mentality for twenty-five years.

That's how long we were married. There were some good times, for sure, but there was rarely balance. Any bliss we experienced was fleeting. I can't pin the blame on just her or me—it was both of us. Our marriage got off to a rocky start as our lives took different trajectories, and we never could recover. I think we scratched each other's itch to love and be loved, but it wasn't deep enough to sustain. We sought to heal our marriage in various ways, though nothing worked.

The source or sources of one's depression can begin to take root years before the depression is actually felt. The origins of mine were plentiful: my father's antics, my mother's aloofness, their crazed marriage, my abnormal high school experience, my move east, and a marriage I wasn't ready for. And that was all just through college. There would be much more to come.

CHAPTER 7

CROSSING THE LINE

In 1987, the NFL draft was not as extravagant as it is today. Back then it was a two-day, twelve-round, unceremonious affair, and that year it took place on a Tuesday and Wednesday in late April, two months after Marshawn and I were married. ESPN aired the draft, but I didn't watch it because I didn't have cable and wasn't on any team's radar. Nobody in the national media interviewed me about it. The Calgary Stampeders of the inferior Canadian Football League were the only team that put me through a workout. And the agent I'd hired was the only one who showed any interest in me.

When my phone rang on the second day of the draft, I was on the couch doing homework.

"Erik, this is Ray Perkins, the new head coach of the Tampa Bay Buccaneers," he said in his southern drawl.

"Oh, hey, Coach," I replied.

"I want you to know that we're looking to take a quarterback in the last round. We have narrowed it down to you and Mike Shula from Alabama."

"Really? That's great. I appreciate the consideration."

It was an honor to speak to Ray, but I'm not exaggerating my lack of enthusiasm during our conversation. First, Mike Shula had the pedigree as the son of legendary NFL coach Don Shula. Second, Alabama was a football powerhouse and NC State wasn't, so their players garnered more attention from scouts than ours. And third, Mike had been the starting quarterback the past three seasons for the Crimson Tide under the school's recently departed head coach: Ray Perkins.

In my mind, it was game, set, and match to Mike—and that's who Tampa Bay ended up drafting.

I wasn't disappointed, though, because I'd never expected to be drafted in the first place. I also believe everything happens for a reason, and not being selected set me on a track to the NFL in the most adventurous way.

It began the morning after the draft, when teams were free to sign undrafted players. My agent called to say that the New Orleans Saints wanted me. He said one scout told him they liked my athleticism and confidence, and the team backed it up by opening its checkbook—sort of. They offered me a two-year contract worth $70,000 the first year and $80,000 the second year, which was contingent on me making the team. They also guaranteed me a $5,000 signing bonus and a modest sum each week I was in training camp. To put my salary into perspective, the average annual pay for a player in 1987 was about $230,000. Quarterback Vinny Testaverde, the first pick in that draft, reportedly signed a six-year, $8.2 million deal. But for me, it was the opportunity that mattered, not the money. Quite frankly, the Saints over-paid. I would've tried out for free.

When I arrived at training camp at Southeastern Louisiana University in Hammond, I learned that I was one of several quarterbacks who'd been invited. NFL teams usually kept three, and veterans Bobby Hebert and Dave Wilson were shoo-ins, so I assumed I was vying for the third spot.

I wasn't.

During the first few days of practice, the coaches barely acknowledged my presence. The only reps I took were for one-on-one pass-rushing drills, meaning that I was essentially a human tackling dummy for linemen with a hundred pounds or more on me. I soon came to realize that they'd signed me as nothing more than a "camp body"—a temporary player used to fill space—a term no player wanted attached to his name. My assess-ment was confirmed during each preseason game when I didn't take a single snap. By the time the Saints released me in late August after the third preseason game, most other teams had set their rosters, so I had no chance of trying out for anyone else.

I left camp with my signing bonus, weekly stipends, and a harsh lesson on the business side of pro football.

I was still a few credit hours short of graduating, so in the fall, I returned to NC State and Marshawn. With no more playing eligibility left, I volunteered to help Coach Sheridan prepare the Wolfpack for the upcoming season. And I was happy. Before the draft, that's where I thought I would be anyway, and now I had some cash in the bank to go with it.

However, at the end of September, two weeks into the NFL season, my life took a wild turn yet again when a representative from the Pittsburgh Steelers called.

"Erik, the players are about to go on strike, but the league will continue playing and we need a quarterback," he said.

Talk of a strike had been simmering for a while, and a rumor that the NFL would still play games if it happened had been floating around for weeks, but few believed it. After all, who would the owners find as replacements?

Now I knew.

Minutes after the Steelers called, the Falcons got ahold of me. Understand that these weren't requests for me to try out. These calls were for me to play—now. I jumped at the chance and chose Atlanta over Pittsburgh, admittedly for their offer of about $7,500 a game, which was more than the Steelers were willing to pay. How could I say no to what would likely be my only chance of ever playing in the NFL? Yes, I realized I would be labeled a "scab" by some players and fans for crossing the picket line, but I didn't care. If I didn't take one of the offers, another player would. Besides, it was temporary—just until the strike ended. Having the regular players—whom I had no relationship with—shun me was worth the risk.

This was a surreal experience that few athletes in any sport have ever had. I went from being undrafted to being cut to being summoned to play immediately, all in about five months. I flew to Atlanta the following day, had less than two weeks to learn the team's playbook, and was in uniform for the next three weeks for home games against the Steelers, San Francisco 49ers, and Rams.

Against the Steelers, I backed up starter Jeff Van Raaphorst and played like a replacement player, completing just 5 of 13 passes for 48 yards and two interceptions. We ended up losing 28–12.

During my first start, which came against the 49ers and Joe Montana (who'd crossed the picket line), I showed improvement, connecting on 13 of 33 passes for 176 yards, including a touchdown and an interception. Despite a second-half comeback, we lost 25–17.

I was finally in the zone the following week against the Rams. I started again and completed 27 of 46 passes for 335 yards with three touchdowns and two interceptions in a 24–20 victory. At the time, the passing attempts, completions, and yards were all single-game franchise rookie records. I also tied Steve Bartkowski and Randy Johnson for passing touchdowns in a game by a rookie. Incredibly, all four records were still standing at the start of the 2023 season.

With most of the regular players on strike, our average attendance for those three games at Fulton County Stadium was about 13,700. (More than 63,000 had attended in week two, the last game before the strike.) Obviously, fans weren't too interested in us. But that didn't deter me. Also, several high-profile players returned before the strike ended, so we weren't strictly using or playing against replacement players, which made my time on the field more meaningful to me.

My biggest challenge was adjusting to the speed of the pro game. The jump in skill level from high school to college is a huge leap; it's even more enormous from college to pro. That's why it took until my third game to kick it up a few notches and settle into a groove. Once I did, and we were successful against the Rams, I knew I could play at that level and deserved to be there. So did the Falcons.

When the strike ended and all the regular players returned, head coach Marion Campbell summoned me to his office. I brought my playbook and set it on his desk, assuming my tenure was over.

"You keep that," he said, sliding it back to me. "We like what we've seen from you and want you with us the rest of the season."

I was shocked. They already had three quarterbacks: Scott Campbell, David Archer, and Chris Miller. I'd never known a team to keep a fourth, but I think the coaches were concerned about the physical and mental effects the layoff might've had on those three. Retaining me at my nominal salary was a low-risk investment.

Of the ten games remaining, we only won once and finished with the league's worst record at 3–12. I didn't play a single down the rest of the season, nor did I care. In the most unorthodox way, I'd made it to the NFL and was happy to have been part of the team. In that short time, I'd learned from some of the best coaches, including offensive coordinator and quarterbacks coach Rod Dowhower, who would go on to coach the quarterbacks for the Washington Redskins during their 1991–92 Super Bowl run; wide receivers coach Jimmy Raye, an offensive coach for thirty-five years with ten different NFL teams; and Jim Hanifan, the offensive line coach who would hold the same job for the 1999–2000 Super Bowl champion St. Louis Rams.

And even though I'd crossed their picket line, the regular Falcons' players never took issue with me. They didn't buddy up to me, but they didn't spurn me either. Indifferent is the best way to describe it. A visual metaphor for my place on the team was evident in the parking lot during practices and home games, where I parked my rusty yellow 1970 Volkswagen Beetle among sleek BMWs, Porsches, and Mercedes-Benzes. We were all football players, but some were considered more valuable than others.

Marshawn had made the move to Atlanta with me, but we separated weeks later due to our failing marriage. Tim Green, a linebacker for the Falcons and the only veteran on the team to cross the picket line, let me stay in his town house during the separation and became a good friend during that time. Remember, this was in the fall of 1987, the same year Marshawn and I were married, before I suggested divorce around Christmas.

Along with that tension, I had to deal with my dad. He was still in North Carolina, unemployed, and searching for a shortcut to prevent his house from going into fore-closure. He eventually asked me for help, and I obliged because I didn't want him or Kelley to suffer. I wrote him a check in late 1987, but I don't know where the money went. He lost the house weeks later, and he and Kelley returned to Southern California.

In the fall of 1988, the Falcons cut me after the third preseason game. They didn't need four quarterbacks anymore, and I was the odd man out. Days after my release, with no other NFL teams calling, the Calgary Stampeders of the CFL—the lone team that worked me out in college before the draft—offered me a two-year contract. So Marshawn and I, back together again, moved north and became honorary Canadians. I played some that season and was slated to be the team's starting quarterback in 1989, but I blew out my knee in a preseason scrimmage and went on the injured list for the entire year. During my recovery and rehab, I made a lot of friends on the team, learned how to fly-fish, and bartended at a place that a teammate's father owned. Playing and hanging out with those guys in Calgary was a highlight of my football days. Many of those on the team were ordinary, middle-class Canadians who played as much for fun as for the modest amount of money they earned.

When my contract expired after the 1989 season, Marshawn and I returned to California. Coming off a severe injury with no job prospects and no agent—even he'd given up on me—I assumed my football career was finished. But with plenty of time on my hands, my knee fully healed. Unsure of what I wanted to do next with my life, a crazy idea came to mind. In January 1990, after the 49ers shellacked the Denver Broncos in the Super Bowl, I found an old NFL media guide in a box of souvenirs from my time with the Falcons. It listed the main office phone numbers for all twenty-eight teams.

"Hi, my name is Erik Kramer. Can I please speak to someone in your personnel department?"

Yes, I called every team in alphabetical order: Atlanta, Buffalo, Chicago. . . . But not to inquire about becoming a coach or joining a front office—I wanted to play. No joke. As ludicrous as it sounds, back then it was the only way for an agentless, mediocre, no-name quarterback to do it. I had to relinquish my pride and expectations and not worry about how much those calls were costing me. Well, maybe I was a little concerned—long-distance calls weren't cheap at the time—but I felt it was worth the investment.

"Sir, let me connect you to our coaching staff's office," was the general answer I received from each reception-ist after explaining who I was.

Among the twenty-eight teams, two coaches actu-ally answered their phones, stifled their laughter as best they could, and politely turned me down. I left messages for the other twenty-six. Only one returned my call, but that's all I needed.

CHAPTER 8

INJURING MY WAY BACK TO THE NFL

On a blustery and bone-chilling February afternoon, an administrative assistant at the Silverdome in Pontiac, Michigan, where the Detroit Lions played and practiced, led me to Mouse Davis's office.

"Mr. Davis will be right with you," she said.

I was nervous. Mouse was the team's offensive coordinator and widely considered the master of the up-tempo run-and-shoot offense. I had cold-called my way into this opportunity, and I had one shot to prove myself to one of the best offensive minds in the game.

When he walked in a few minutes later, he seemed startled to see someone in his office. "Oh, hi. Can I help you?"

"Hi, Coach. Erik Kramer," I said, standing to shake his hand. Mouse hesitantly extended his hand to accept mine.

"I'm sorry, who?" he replied.

"Erik Kramer. You flew me in for a workout today."

Mouse looked confused.

"I was told you guys are looking for another quarterback," I said.

"Yeah, we are," Mouse responded, dragging his words with a tone of uncertainty. "But I don't know anything about a workout."

Well, this is awkward.

"We may have to have you come back," he said. "Where did you come in from?"

"California," I replied. "Los Angeles."

"Hmm. Okay. That's a long way to come. The problem is the turf is torn up for a tractor show," he said. "But hang on a sec."

Mouse left the room and returned with June Jones, the quarterbacks and wide receivers coach. June introduced himself and, thank goodness, he was expecting me.

As I would learn many years later from June, he had thought highly of me when I was at NC State. As the Houston Oilers' quarterbacks coach in 1987, June had evaluated me before draft day as a "make it" guy—someone the Oilers should strongly consider drafting—but the Oilers front office didn't listen to him. When June got to Detroit in 1989, the Lions needed another quarterback, so he mentioned me to members of the front office, which, coincidentally, must've been around the same time I was calling teams. June set up a workout session for me but didn't tell Mouse until I arrived. Mouse had been tending to other player issues, so June didn't want to distract him.

"Sorry about the mix-up and the field situation here," June said to me. "Are you okay riding with us to the University of Michigan? It's about an hour away, but we can work you out there."

"Absolutely," I replied.

With a bag of footballs in tow, we piled into Mouse's Cadillac and headed southwest to Ann Arbor. The nerves I'd felt when I arrived dissipated during our drive as we casually talked about football and the highlights of my college and pro careers. Granted, there weren't many, but there were enough to interest them and keep the car rolling toward Ann Arbor. I was actually glad Mouse didn't know about my visit in advance. That meant he had no preconceived expectations and knew nothing about me besides the good things I told him.

When we arrived at Michigan's Oosterbaan Field House, I had no receivers to throw to, so June pointed to places on the field for me to hit with my throws—and I was spot-on. I would've knocked over a soda can fifty yards away nine out of ten times. To say they were impressed is an understatement. They weren't about to hand me the starting job, but they knew they might've found a second- or third-string quarterback to give them some depth.

After the forty-minute workout, we drove back to the Silverdome where June and Mouse met with Chuck Schmidt, the general manager, before calling me in. Chuck offered me a two-year deal on the spot and an invitation to their minicamp in Florida in March. The contract was contingent on me making the team. My salary would be $200,000 for the first year and $225,000 in the second, a significant increase compared to my contracts with the Saints and Falcons.

The result of my effort to phone all twenty-eight teams reminded me of the sobering lesson I'd learned at Pierce when I was beat out at quarterback and behaved like a jerk: don't let your ego overshadow your goal. I had to swallow my pride, put in the work, and take the bad with the good. Although, I could've saved money on my long-distance phone bill if I'd known to stop calling teams after getting through the *D*'s in the media guide.

I held my own at Detroit's minicamp with veteran quarterbacks Rodney Peete and Bob Gagliano, and I felt good about my chances of making the team. But then the draft happened in late April.

With the team's first pick, the Lions selected quarterback Andre Ware, the Heisman Trophy winner who'd employed the same run-and-shoot offense at the University of Houston. *What are they doing?* I wondered. *They already have Rodney and Bob. Where do I fit into this?* I didn't. It was the "camp body" scenario with New Orleans all over again.

But, as you've seen, there's usually a sharp twist or turn to steer my story onto an unforeseen course.

The door that apparently had been slammed shut in my face sprung open when Andre and the Lions couldn't agree on a contract. I'd thought the only chance I had to make the team was if someone got hurt, which I didn't wish on any of those guys. But Andre's holdout reshaped everything. He missed the start of training camp in late July and nearly all of August, not signing until late that month when we were deep into the preseason. That gave me enough time to prove myself—which I did.

Our third preseason game was at home against the Kansas City Chiefs. During pregame warm-ups, one of the front office guys approached me.

"Erik, we need you to fake an injury tonight," he said. I laughed. He didn't.

"Wait, you're serious?"

"Yeah, I'm serious," he replied. "We want to keep you. The problem is we don't have room on the roster, so we need you to go on the injured list."

The rules for the injured list and other roster designations are different today, but back then, this was something teams did to keep players. By pretending to get hurt, I would be ineligible to play unless another quarterback got injured for real—but I'd be a Lion. When I initially thought my only chance to make the team was if someone got hurt, I never thought it would be me. This wasn't what I'd had in mind for my NFL comeback, but I was certain that no other team would want me if I were cut, so I agreed to take a dive.

In the second half, with the ball on the Chiefs' five-yard line, I planned to roll out, throw the ball, and come up limping. It would look like a simple twisted ankle that I could blame on the artificial turf. But I didn't need to because as I rolled out, a defender leapfrogged my blocker and hammered me to the ground, separating my shoulder. I was legitimately in severe pain and was placed on the injured list the next day. It was an agonizing turn of events but an honest one that secured my job.

Although I remained on the injured list all season, I attended every game, participated in team meetings, and practiced when healthy. We finished 6–10 but had a solid core of players heading into 1991. My goal was to be part of it on the field every Sunday.

As excited as I was to be back in the NFL, Marshawn and I continued to struggle. I didn't recognize it then, but we had become my parents—as incompatible as water and oil. We remained on two different paths and out of sync. While I knew that divorce was still probably best for both of us, I felt compelled to keep trying. Why? For the same reason I kept trying after proposing divorce ten months into our marriage. One could argue this time that three-plus years was enough of an effort, but overcoming obstacles had become part of who I was. How could I not conquer this? I couldn't quit, at least not yet. Divorce would be accepting a defeat I couldn't undo, and I hated losing with a passion.

Good God, I was becoming my mother.

Prior to the 1991 season and desperate to find a solution, one day I approached Dr. Keith Burch, an internist with the Lions. "My wife and I have been having problems for years," I said. "Could you recommend a good marriage counselor?"

Without hesitation, he referred me to Dr. Kevin Wildenhaus.

CHAPTER 9

THE POWER OF THERAPY

Dr. Wildenhaus is a clinical psychologist, and from my experience, one of the best in the business. In the 1990s, he was an outpatient therapist at Henry Ford Health Center and the team psychologist for the Lions. In 2001, he became the team psychologist for the Steelers and later for the Pittsburgh Penguins hockey team, and he continues in those roles today. He also serves as the behavioral science leader for Janssen research and development, a division of Johnson & Johnson. On the football side, he attends combines, administers psychological tests to potential players, is involved in draft meetings, and offers his expertise to executives on draft day. He also works with players on mental skills training and helping them reach their peak performance.

Marshawn and I attended about half a dozen sessions together with Dr. Wildenhaus. Each visit was in a refreshingly calm and polite environment, which was the direct opposite of our home life. Through his honest yet sensitive approach, Dr. Wildenhaus taught us empathy by understanding how our words and actions affected each other. In an attempt to explain our present issues, he also dug deep into our pasts to unearth our origins and learn who we were as individuals. Meeting with him helped us in the short term, but nothing stuck. Marshawn and I could each offer our own reasons why it didn't work—some we'd agree on and some we would not—but I know Dr. Wildenhaus wasn't the problem. That's because I continued to see him by myself to try to straighten out my football career, and what he did was nothing short of a miracle.

After my shoulder healed, I began practicing with the Lions midway through the 1990 season, but I struggled mightily. The problem was mental, not physical. I watched a lot of film, studied the team playbook, and worked one-on-one with receivers, but that extra effort didn't produce results in practice. As I'd learned in Atlanta, the NFL game is exceedingly fast. But this time, I couldn't get my brain to slow down to process the action around me. It affected my timing, accuracy, and decisions. It had also become difficult to let go of my mistakes. I carried them from one play to the next as they snowballed into disarray. After the season, with the 1991 campaign approaching, I needed to do something if I had any shot at making the team.

Enter Dr. Wildenhaus.

After assessing my state of mind through numerous questions and discussions over a few sessions, he asked me if I'd ever heard of "mindfulness." The therapy technique helps one concentrate on the present through meditation, breathing, and visualization. I hadn't, but

I was willing to try anything. In the western world in 1990, mindfulness was not a mainstream concept like it is today. The notion of it in pop culture was little more than a decade old, but Dr. Wildenhaus was already an expert on it.

Recently, I talked to Dr. Wildenhaus, and he spoke candidly about the direction he took with me:

"A big part of my focus with you was to quiet your mind so that you could get the voice out of your head—the voice we all have—the one trying to judge and analyze and critique everything we do. I did it by teaching you breathing exercises and very simple visualization techniques. For example, there's so much chaos around a quarterback—the defensive linemen attacking, linebackers blitzing, receivers adjusting their routes. And while all that's happening, the clock in your head is counting 'one thousand one, one thousand two . . . ,' so you get rid of the ball quickly and on time. I helped you be aware of the chaos but not distracted by it."

He started by taking me on a ride.

"I told you to imagine yourself on an inflatable inner tube, floating down a river," Dr. Wildenhaus said. "As you're moving, you come upon giant rocks of all shapes on every side. Any one of these rocks can flip you or puncture the tube, so you need to be aware of the dangers the rocks pose but navigate around them and not be distracted by them. It's the same as when you're playing quarterback and you drop your head in an attempt to escape pressure rather than keeping your eyes downfield on your receivers. Your goal is to get down that river, and you can do it successfully if you keep your focus and eliminate the distractions."

I was skeptical that something seemingly as simple as mindfulness could fix my game, but after a few weeks of trying it, I was reformed. The combination of meditating, breathing, and visualizing before and during practices—and, eventually, games—enabled me to break down the chaos in my mind and reassemble the pieces in an organized and composed manner. I was suddenly firing on all cylinders on the field and playing outstanding football with unwavering confidence.

I also tried mindfulness at home with Marshawn. Yes, it's a bit more challenging when you're doing it on your own for a problem that involves two people. But even though she was unaware I was practicing it in her presence, it made some of my worst days a bit brighter. And, in turn, maybe hers. This is why I recommend that anyone who's suffering from depression or is in a mental funk of any kind give mindfulness a chance. It may not solve all your problems, but it can help you think more clearly and see your world in a more positive light.

The purpose of the first practice of mindfulness—meditating—is to settle the mind and calm the nerves. As Dr. Wildenhaus put it, "You want to be like a car in neutral"—the engine is idling smoothly but not too revved up. With balance comes focus. During one of our sessions, he asked me, "If I told you there's something outside my office door that will make you feel entirely comfortable and relaxed, what would it look like?" After I described something personal to him, he said, "Now lay back, close your eyes, and I'll take you to that place." And he did just that, softly speaking as I savored the journey in my mind's eye. It wasn't hypnosis, but I felt like I'd traveled to another dimension for a few minutes. When I opened my eyes, my mind was at ease, refreshed, and energized. Meditating away from his office, which I did with my own voice in my mind or with cassette tapes he'd recorded, helped me filter out distractions, trust my abilities, and zero in on the task in front of me.

Breathing, the second practice, is something we usually see as physical rather than connected to our minds. In a game, a tense situation might cause my heart to pound faster and my blood pressure to rise, negatively affecting my concentration. Dr. Wildenhaus taught me to focus on my breathing to counteract that stress and maintain the neutral state I'd established through meditation. For example, he suggested that before each game I pick out a fixed object in the stadium—like an advertisement or the American flag—that would serve, at any moment, as my reminder to breathe. When I felt tense, I would look at that fixture and it would cue me to take a breath and slow down my mind.

In another example, he noticed that I always got down on one knee in the huddle when calling the play, which is something a lot of quarterbacks did back in the day. As a way to remember to let go of the previous play, he told me to swipe my fingers along the grass each time

I knelt. This allowed me to let go of the last play, center myself again, and regain control of my faculties before calling the next play.

The third practice, visualization, involves picturing a situation and its potential outcomes before it's set in motion. This can help a person adjust on the spot. In my case, Dr. Wildenhaus had me visualize my coaches sending in a play. Before learning visualization, my process was to give the play to my teammates, look over the defense, and hope everything worked as planned. With visualization, I envisioned the play unfolding in its entirety, its possible obstacles, and what I wanted it to accomplish—all before snapping the ball. As we broke the huddle and jogged to the line of scrimmage, my eyes were like camera lenses zooming in and out and panning from side to side while my brain methodically processed the information. I reviewed the ABCs that every quarterback should: Are my teammates lined up correctly? Is the defensive coverage man-to-man or zone? Is someone going to blitz? If so, which of my linemen or running backs will block him?

Then I delved deeper: If the play works as designed, what should I expect to happen? A completed pass? Touchdown? And what adjustments should I make to produce the result I want? Practicing this made me feel psychic in a sense. It gave me control by slowing the game's pace and helping me more accurately anticipate the result.

I'd spent two seasons as an NFL player before I met Dr. Wildenhaus. One was as a replacement player who didn't take a single snap after the strike was over. The other was on the injured list. In other words, my career was essentially nonexistent. After I met Dr. Wildenhaus, it completely transformed me as a professional football player.

My only regret with therapy is that the sessions Marshawn and I had with Dr. Wildenhaus didn't work for us. Sometimes therapy is successful; other times, it's not. And the reasons, in either case, can vary. I can't fault the effort she and I made to get help, but we couldn't execute what we'd learned. What effect, if any, this had on my eventual depression, I can't say, nor do I dwell on it. It's just unfortunate that we could never gain our footing together.

CHAPTER 10

BRASS

After a strong training camp in the summer of 1991, I made the team and vaulted to second on the depth chart behind Rodney. Andre was third. Bob had signed with the San Diego Chargers during the offseason. I was physically and mentally sharper than I could ever recall. I went from the injured list to beating out the team's number one draft pick. And I responded when thrown into action.

In the fourth regular-season game, which was against the Indianapolis Colts, Rodney was injured on a third-down play with about six minutes left in the third quarter. It was nothing serious, and with a punt forthcoming, he could get the quick treatment and rest he needed without missing a play. But our punt pinned the Colts inside their one-yard line, and on their first play, we tackled running back Eric Dickerson in the end zone for a safety. As a result, the Colts had to punt to us on the next play, and we returned it to their thirty-six-yard line. Rodney wasn't ready to return yet.

"Kramer! You're in!" Coach Wayne Fontes hollered.

My adrenaline spiked as I snagged my helmet off the bench and sprinted onto the field. When I got to the huddle, I remembered to throw my brain into neutral to relax. If I hadn't, my first pass surely would've ripped through the roof of the Hoosier Dome. Instead, I completed a sixteen-yard pass over the middle to receiver Brett Perriman for a first down. That was followed by a couple of short gains, giving us a third down and one on the Colts' eleven-yard line. The call from the sidelines was to give the ball to superstar running back Barry Sanders.

Barry Sanders ranks among the greatest running backs in the game's history. If you never saw him play, it's worth the time to watch videos of him. Many guys in the NFL are freaks of nature, but not Barry. At the time, he was five eight and about two hundred pounds. He didn't plow through defenders—he danced and spun around them, sprinted past them, and made them look like they'd never played football before. It wasn't unusual for him to have forty- or fifty-yard bursts or more without being touched. And what I loved most about him was his humility. He was as quiet in the huddle as he appeared in interviews. He was one of the few players who would politely hand the ball to an official after scoring a touchdown rather than showboating. His idea of celebrating was to go to the bench, drape his head with a towel, and sit alone while waiting for his next turn on the field. Even though the 1991 season was just his third in the league, I knew he was destined for the Hall of Fame.

So with us facing that third down and one, giving the ball to Barry—even with every Colt knowing he would get it—was the only sensible call to make. Unless you

That's me communicating with Barry Sanders in a game against the Washington Redskins. *(Photo courtesy: Detroit Lions)*

were a new quarterback thrown into the game and suddenly suffered a brain cramp.

When we broke the huddle and stepped to the line of scrimmage, I scanned the defense. I immediately saw a one-on-one matchup with wide receiver Willie Green to my left that was to our advantage given Willie's height. Armed with my visualization technique, I envisioned hitting Willie with a quick pass in the front left corner of the end zone near the pylon. Willie saw it too and signaled me with his right hand to get him the ball. So I called an audible, took the snap, did a short four-step drop, and threw the ball to the exact spot I'd pictured. It worked to perfection. Touchdown, Kramer to Green!

After a brief on-field celebration, I jogged to the sidelines toward offensive line coach Jerry Wampfler. He had his head down and his hands on his knees.

"Kramer!" he shouted as he lifted his head. "You shouldn't be allowed on the plane ride home!"

"What? Why not?" It was like I was speaking to Coach Crow in high school all over again.

"Because you took the ball out of Barry Sanders's hands on third down and short!"

I was dumbfounded. *What's he talking about? Yeah, I changed the play, but . . .* I continued toward the bench where Willie was sitting.

"Hey, Willie!" I exclaimed. "Did you know that was third down?"

Willie stared at me in disbelief.

"Huh," I said. "I could've sworn it was second down."

Despite my lapse in judgment, I completed the two passes I threw, including the one for a touchdown. Rodney played the rest of the way as we defeated the Colts 33–24 for our third win in a row.

When we boarded the bus following the game, an offensive lineman called to me from the back.

"Hey, Brass!" he bellowed, waving his hand. "Come sit with us!" He called me Brass, as in "brass balls," for having the guts to throw on third and one with Barry lined up behind me. I didn't see a reason to tell him that I didn't know what down it was and shouldn't have called that audible. I'd earned myself a fabulous nickname and the respect of my teammates.

Five weeks later, with a record of 5–2, we were tied atop the NFC Central Division with the Bears. But while playing the Dallas Cowboys in late October, we were dealt a severe blow when Rodney suffered a torn Achilles tendon early on in the game. He'd been having his best year as a pro, and it was now on me to keep the train moving full steam ahead. Tied 0–0 when Rodney was helped off the field, our coaches called a conservative game the rest of the way, not wanting to throw me to the wolves. We amassed just 208 yards of total offense but won handily, 34–10. I completed 9 of 16 passes for 108 yards and two touchdowns, while our defense and special teams produced critical scoring plays.

"I feel I gained a little bit of respect and confidence from my teammates and the coaching staff," I told *Washington Post* reporter David Aldridge after the game. "Hopefully, we can go on from here and just take them as they come. I feel prepared. I guess if I feel any pressure, it's welcomed."

I went on to start the rest of the season, which had everyone in Detroit on edge for the first couple weeks. We lost 20–10 during my first start, which was played in Chicago in eighteen-degree weather. My second start was a disaster; we lost 30–21 in Tampa Bay to the lowly Buccaneers, who were 1–8.

Our next game came against the Rams at home, and we continued to struggle for the first three quarters. We were down 10–7 in the fourth when I connected with wide receiver Robert Clark for a touchdown—but one of our offensive linemen, right guard Mike Utley, went down after the play.

"It was the eleventh game of the season, first play of the fourth quarter," Mike told mlive.com reporter Eric

Woodyard nearly twenty-five years later, in 2016. "Erik Kramer comes back and gets us in the huddle and it's a 7-step drop throw pass. At that time, we were behind the Rams point-wise, but we were better than the Rams on that Sunday."

Mike was blocking Rams' defensive linemen David Rocker. It was a clean play by Rocker.

"I went to take his legs out to catch him and knock him so he [had] to defend me and not the ball," Mike said. "He put his hands on my shoulder, hit me, and knocked me down. Right then and there, I hit my head, I broke my neck, and I knew I was in trouble."

I ran to the sidelines after the touchdown and initially didn't know Mike had been hurt. Even when I saw him down and being put on a stretcher, I didn't realize how bad it was. In fact, it wasn't until the next day, when a group of us visited him at the hospital, that we learned he'd suffered a spinal cord injury and was paralyzed from the waist down.

As the medical staff carted Mike off the field, he gave the crowd a thumbs-up with his right hand. Many players do that today when they're seriously injured, but Mike might've been the first. His gesture, which became a symbol for the Mike Utley Foundation that he started the following year, brought the crowd to its feet and got our adrenaline pumping.

"It was a tragedy of epic proportions," Bill Keenist, the Lions' public relations director from 1987 to 2017, recently said to me. "It would turn out to be a very emotional rallying point for the team and our fans. In fact, during our playoff game later that season against Dallas, John Madden commented that every team is confronted with emotional hurdles, but the question is, 'How will you handle it?' And our guys couldn't have handled it any better."

That pivotal day, we scored another touchdown and beat the Rams, 21–10. With a 7–4 record, five regular-season games left, and Mike heavy on our minds, we were determined to win for him. And we did. We won all five games, including one against each of our division rivals: the Bears, Minnesota Vikings, and Green Bay Packers. We finished the regular season 12–4 and captured the division title.

While Mike's injury was a catalyst for our success, many people—even those within the Lions' organization—were surprised that we could do it with me at the helm. I didn't post huge numbers, but I didn't need to with the talent around me. Kevin Colbert, who retired in 2022 after twenty years as the general manager for the Steelers, was our director of pro scouting in 1991.

"What you were able to do certainly was a bit of a shock, but as things continued to click with you, we just kept riding it," Kevin told me years later. "You were one of those players where it's sometimes difficult for others to see what you've got until you're in a competitive situation. You didn't have ideal speed, size, athleticism, or arm strength, but your intelligence and toughness were well documented. Those intangibles superseded your tangibles. That's why you were an NFL quarterback."

Those twelve wins, still the most in the franchise's ninety-plus years going into the 2023 season, set us up for a rematch against Dallas in the playoffs. The Cowboys ended the regular season with five straight victories and won their wild card playoff game in Chicago. The Las Vegas sports books showed us no respect by listing our game with them as even, meaning they thought the Cowboys, who were dubbed "America's Team," had as good a chance to win as we did, despite us being at home and beating them by twenty-four points in week nine.

We showed America otherwise.

We destroyed the Cowboys, 38–6. The coaches unleashed me this time as I finished 29 of 38 for 341 yards and three touchdowns. Detroit fans still remember this game fondly. And even though the Cowboys later went on to win three Super Bowls in the 1990s, their fans also haven't forgotten it. We beat them in every facet. My visualization technique had never worked with such precision. I felt like I knew everything that would happen before it happened. While watching a replay of the game, I noticed that my facial expression and demeanor never changed. On our first drive, John Madden said, "Erik Kramer, I'll tell ya . . . [he's] as cool as you can be in a playoff game." Now you know why. I was asked why the magnitude of the game didn't rattle me. By practicing mindfulness throughout, the big stage and bright lights were irrelevant. I was prepared for everything Dallas threw at me from start to finish.

Cowboys' linebacker Jack Del Rio was one of several players who constantly tried to unnerve me. He called me a scab before the game for crossing the picket line four years earlier and continued to jaw at me play after play, claiming I wasn't going to hold up under pressure. In a *Chicago Tribune* article by Don Pierson, Jack said after the game, "No way did we think he could do that. I just saw him do it, and I still don't think he can do it."

Dallas cornerback Issiac Holt told the *Tribune*, "Everyone says he's only this or only that. The guy can play."

And then there was defensive tackle Tony Casillas, who the *Tribune* said referred to me as a scab quarterback. Tony was one of the Falcons' players on strike that season who became my teammate when the strike ended.

"Something in my life I had to do," I collectedly told the reporter who informed me of Tony's comment. I understood why Tony held a grudge, but I made no apology then and still don't make one today. I mentioned that Joe Montana and some other high profile veterans had crossed the picket line. They included the likes of Lawrence Taylor, Tony Dorsett, Howie Long, Roger Craig, Steve Largent, and Ozzie Newsome. The players who did not cross the picket line, like Tony Casillas, opened a door for me. All I did was walk through it and make the most of it.

We were one win from going to the Super Bowl, but Washington stood in our way. The Redskins finished the regular season with the league's best record at 14–2. Led by future Hall of Fame coach Joe Gibbs and Pro Bowl quarterback Mark Rypien, they had pummeled us 45–0 in the season's opening week. But Barry Sanders didn't play that game due to an injury. We were a much better team with him healthy.

CHAPTER 11

ALL ABOUT DAD

The victory over Dallas was the Lions' first playoff win since 1957. The city was euphoric, and the nation was stunned. After the game, Rick Telander wrote the following for *Sports Illustrated*:

"Quarterback Erik Kramer, whose junior college team, Los Angeles Pierce, lost to Taft College 51–24 in the 1983 Potato Bowl, was so terrific that reporters didn't know quite what to ask him when it was all over.

"'Can you throw like that all the time?'

"'Yes.'

"'Didn't the Cowboy and the Lion helmets look alike to you?'

"'No.'

"'You played at Virginia, right?'"

Rick ended the article with this:

"'All year long people have given us no respect,' said Kramer. He smiled, then added, 'That's Erik. With a K.'"

I loved it. And I honestly didn't care if nobody knew who I was. As long as Detroiters were happy, I was happy. The Tigers had won a World Series in 1984, and the Pistons had won NBA titles in 1989 and 1990, but the

Lions had experienced a thirty-five-year drought in the playoffs. Not anymore.

Sometime midweek, before we left for Washington, our communications director Bill Keenist called me at home and asked me to stop by his office the next morning before practice to discuss a media issue. Several of us had given local and national interviews that week, so I assumed this was about another request. It was, but I couldn't believe the subject matter.

"Pat O'Brien from CBS called," Bill said. "They've interviewed your dad and want to talk to you."

"My dad? Why?" I asked with trepidation in my voice.

Dad wasn't on my speed dial. In fact, we hadn't spoken in quite a long time. I'd heard from family that he'd left Southern California and moved to Las Vegas, supposedly to drive a cab in his latest effort to earn a living. I didn't even know if he was still there or had moved on to his next venture.

"I guess your dad told them he's homeless and living in a high school coach's garage in Los Angeles," Bill said. I just shook my head. "Pat wants to tell you what your dad said and give you a chance to comment."

Many athletes respected Pat, who'd been with CBS Sports since the early 1980s. I called him when we got to Washington a few days before the game, and he was very polite about the matter. Pat's impression of Dad was that he was seeking sympathy by trying to convey an image that he had nothing despite his son's success. Pat promised to balance my perspective with Dad's. I wasn't upset with Pat for doing his job. I was disappointed in my dad for still being Dad—worried only about himself and oblivious to how his actions affected others. I called Dad as soon as Pat and I hung up.

"Dad, it's Erik," I said tersely.

"Oh, hey, Erik!"

"What did you do?" I snapped.

"Huh? What are you talking about?"

"You know *exactly* what I'm talking about!"

"Erik, it wasn't me!" he insisted.

"How was it not you?"

"*They* came to *me*!" he argued. "I thought they wanted to talk about you and how great you've been doing. I didn't know they would make it about my situation."

His lie exasperated me.

"You know what, Dad?" I said, lowering my voice. "Even if they did come to you, you chose what to say. You could've told them everything I've done to try to help you, but you didn't."

Dad mumbled a few things in his weak defense before I hung up. Nothing had changed. I was still dealing with a child—except that he was in his late forties. It was a prime illustration of the addiction to chaos that Dad needed to function and the lengths he'd take to stir up drama.

We went into Washington's RFK Stadium confident and happy to play the underdog role that we'd been playing all season. But on our first possession, Pro Bowl defensive end Charles Mann, who had eleven and a half sacks that season, smashed me from behind and forced a fumble. The Redskins recovered the ball at the nine-yard line and scored less than a minute into the game. Although we regained our composure and were down only 17–10 at the half, the Redskins pulled away in the third quarter and coasted to a 41–10 win. Two weeks later, they thumped Buffalo in the Super Bowl, winning 37–24.

I don't blame my dad for the loss; he wasn't even remotely on my mind during the game. I was focused and ready. I finished the game 21 of 33 for 249 yards with a touchdown and an interception. We lost the game at the line of scrimmage. The Redskins sacked me four times, and Barry was held to forty-four yards rushing. We lost because arguably one of the best teams in NFL history beat us. They lost only two games that season by a total of five points. They averaged thirty points per game and allowed an average of fourteen, including three shutouts. Other than the 1994–95 49ers, who won Super Bowl XXIX, this Washington team was the best I'd ever seen.

After the season, the Lions rewarded me with another two-year contract with roughly the same terms as my previous one. I knew I would likely return as Rodney's backup, and I was content with that. While some quarterbacks competing for the same job may not get along, Rodney and I had forged a solid friendship. We were about putting the team first and were willing to do whatever was best for the Lions. More than anything, I was happy that football was still part of my life. One, because I loved the game, and two, because it allowed me to compartmentalize issues I had outside of football.

To perform as a professional quarterback, most of my time each day had to be focused on my craft, whether training, practicing, studying, playing, or just thinking about the next game. Yet, I still had to deal with the same human conditions as everyone else. When one of those conditions arose—say, a conflict with Marshawn— I'd address it as quickly and simply as possible and then compartmentalize it to focus on football. That's why the sport was so integral to my mental health. It regularly provided me with a diversion from anything outside the game that was weighing on my mind.

Of course, such a diversion could only last for so long.

Over time, the pressure and stress from our discordant marriage became too much for even professional football to mask. During training camp in July and August of 1992, I decided that sometime after the season started in September, I would ask Marshawn for a divorce. But several highly emotional events on and off the field diverted my plan. It began with shocking news from Marshawn in late September and culminated with a situation beyond my control that wreaked havoc on my brain until the depression finally engulfed me.

CHAPTER 12

FROM MY SON'S BIRTH
TO AN HERBALIST

About three games into the 1992 season, I came home from practice one afternoon and could tell something was on Marshawn's mind. She didn't waste a moment sharing her news.

"Erik," she said. "I'm pregnant."

If you tossed happiness, sadness, excitement, fear, and a host of other emotions into a jar and shook it up like a snow globe, that was the turmoil swirling around in my head. I felt a marvelous sensation from head to toe at the thought of being a father. Yet the notion of bringing a child into our marriage frightened me. This was the woman I was preparing to separate from and divorce for the good of both of us. What now?

As the emotions settled a couple days later, I came to the same conclusion that I did each time I'd considered splitting with Marshawn: everything will be fine. Instead of, "How can we possibly stay married?" I tried to shift my attitude to, "Somehow, we will make this work." I wanted to see her in a different light—not as the woman I couldn't get along with, but as the mother of my child. I thought maybe this was the spark our relationship needed. In hindsight, this way of thinking was foolish beyond measure. The idea that adding a child to our toxic formula would improve our situation is a common mistake many struggling couples make. But what other stance could I take at this point? We were having a baby.

The notion of being a dad also put football into perspective, which I desperately needed that season. When I'd arrived at spring minicamp six months earlier, I was stunned to find that I was third on the depth chart. When I say that I found out at camp, I mean on the field the first day when Rodney and Andre took reps ahead of me. Nobody, including head coach Wayne Fontes, had said anything to me directly. I learned from Kevin Colbert many years later that the team wanted to open up the competition to see where it would lead. They knew what I could do but still didn't know what they had in Andre since he'd held out most of training camp the previous year. They also needed to see how well Rodney had recuperated from his Achilles injury. In addition, we had a new offensive coordinator in Dan Henning. I understand all of that today, but just a couple months removed from knocking on the door of the Super Bowl, it didn't sit well with me.

With the lesson I'd learned a decade earlier at Pierce still fresh in my mind, I worked my butt off, and by the start of the season, I'd put myself on equal ground with Andre in the eyes of the coaches. We played relatively the same amount of time as Rodney's backups and finished the year with comparable stats. Unfortunately, the season as a whole was a colossal disappointment. We lost six games by six points or less, finished 5–11, and came in last in the division. Barry was our shining star, rushing for 1,352 yards.

Marshawn and I moved back to Southern California during the offseason to escape the harsh Detroit winter while she was pregnant. It was the most amicable we'd been in years as we anticipated our child's birth. Her pregnancy went well, and there was a glimmer of hope that things would improve between us.

Griffen was born in Burbank on June 24, 1993, a beautiful boy who appeared healthy in every respect. But

Me, Mom, Griffen, and my grandma. *(Photo courtesy: Erik Kramer)*

within a couple weeks, we knew something was gravely wrong. Griffen cried a lot. I mean *a lot*, and it was affecting his breathing. We took him to one pediatrician. Then another. And another. "It's colic," they all said. But even as amateur parents, we sensed it was something worse. We finally found a doctor who referred us to a specialist, who, in turn, sent us to a hospital for multiple tests.

They kept Griffen overnight and took him into surgery the following morning. He was diagnosed with necrotizing fasciitis, a rare, flesh-eating, bacterial disease that can spread quickly throughout the body. Hearing the word *flesh-eating* was enough for us to know our son was in pain and his life was in danger.

Marshawn and I essentially lived at the hospital for the next six weeks. Griffen had to undergo more surgeries and be put into a medically induced coma and hooked up to a ventilator to help his fragile body heal. I ended up missing all of training camp and didn't return to Detroit until the start of the season, after doctors cleared Griffen to go home and around-the-clock nursing care was in place. The Lions couldn't have been more sympathetic, keeping me on the roster and letting me fly to California on several occasions in September and October. In November, when Griffen was cured and allowed to travel, Marshawn brought him to Detroit where we reunited as a family.

Marshawn and I once again met with Dr. Wildenhaus a few times—not directly for our marriage but more to help us release some of the emotions and heavy hearts we'd carried during Griffen's battle. These sessions proved to be much more beneficial than our previous ones together. I'd faced some challenges throughout my life—mentally with my parents, physically on the field, emotionally with Marshawn—but none of that compared to watching my son go through hell. Many parents know how helpless it feels to watch a child suffer and have no means to control the situation. Marshawn and I would've both traded places with Griffen in a heartbeat, and it was excruciating that we couldn't. We were fortunate that our family made it through and hopeful that we would never have to experience such agony again.

Having Griffen and Marshawn in Detroit was an enormous boost for my psyche. I started the final four games of the season after Rodney was injured in early December. We won three of them, including a season-ending 30–20 win over Green Bay in which our defense picked off Brett Favre four times. That set up a wild card playoff game at home against Favre and the Packers the following week.

Up 17–14 late in the third quarter and deep in Green Bay's territory, I threw the ball toward tight end Ty Hallock in the end zone. But Packers' safety George Teague intercepted my pass and returned it 101 yards for a touchdown. Instead of us going up by ten points, the Packers took a 21–17 lead into the fourth quarter. Among my NFL lowlights, that pick ranks at the top. I shook it off, though, and brought us back with an eighty-nine-yard touchdown drive, giving us a 24–21 lead with a couple minutes left in the game. But Brett Favre tossed a forty-yard touchdown to Sterling Sharpe with less than a minute left for a 28–24 win. We dominated the Packers in total yards, first downs, and time of possession, but they won the stat that mattered.

And just like that, my tenure in Detroit was over.

"You were a free agent. We knew you wanted to test the market, and we respected that," Kevin Colbert later told me. "It wasn't like we didn't want to keep you, but we weren't going to make an offer first because we didn't know what the market was for you. We agreed to stay in touch—let you go out and see what you could get. In the meantime, we'd be looking at other quarterbacks as well."

Fortunately, I didn't have to break out the old media guide again to find another job because the Bears contacted my agent and made it clear up front that they wanted me. In February 1994, Marshawn and I flew to Chicago to meet with head coach Dave Wannstedt.

"Erik, we want to make you this offer," Dave said. "We want you to be the guy to lead the Bears back to glory."

It was a three-year deal worth $8.1 million.

Marshawn and I managed to keep calm throughout the meeting, but when we returned to our hotel room, we held hands and jumped on the bed. Really. Like kids on Christmas morning. I didn't seek any other offers, including from Detroit. My mind was made up.

"The day the Bears made you an offer was the same day we brought in free agent Scott Mitchell from the

Miami Dolphins," Kevin said. "When you immediately agreed to Chicago's terms, that shifted things for us. We knew we had to sign Scott."

Rodney and Andre were also free agents and not expected to return to the Lions. Rodney ended up going to the Cowboys to be Troy Aikman's backup, and Andre signed with the Los Angeles Raiders. Two weeks after I signed with the Bears, Scott signed with Detroit. He would be their starter for the next four years.

The value of my contract mattered little. Family and friends are well aware of my frugality. Materially, I've lived the same with money as I did without it. What the deal did, though, was give me a sense of legitimacy. I wasn't going to be a fill-in for an injured player or expected to hold the ship together until someone better came along. I'd finally made it to the top. I was *the* guy, no longer the underdog I'd been since high school, and it was a fantastic feeling. But at the same time . . . well, I was no longer the underdog I'd been since high school. In other words, the heat had been turned up and everything mattered now—what I did, what I said, how I played. Playing a professional sport is pressure-packed every day. It's like walking a tightrope. You need to have balance and always stay focused. The slightest misstep can cost you your job or career. There were never five minutes when I felt like I had job security in the NFL. You're either moving forward or backward, and that's a daily feeling. Now, as a highly paid quarterback with enormous expectations on my shoulder pads, that tightrope was significantly higher. I welcomed the challenge, but I had to be careful to look straight ahead and not down.

With Griffen healthy, a new contract, and a vibrant city excited to welcome Marshawn and me, I had a great training camp and carried that momentum into our season opener, a 21–9 victory over Tampa Bay. A week later in Philadelphia, we lost a tough one to the Eagles, 30–22, on Monday Night Football.

Then came the nightmare.

Playing Minnesota on our home turf, we were down 10–0 at the half before giving up eighteen more points in the third quarter. That's when Vikings' future Hall of Famer John Randle busted through the line and tossed me hard to the ground, separating my right shoulder. Despite the pain, I sucked it up and stayed in the game, even throwing a touchdown pass to Tom Waddle late in the fourth quarter.

"We'll probably know more as the week goes along. We'll just have to take it day to day," I told a *Tribune* reporter in the locker room afterward. "I think it's just a slight separation. It feels pretty good. Once some of the swelling goes down, things should get even better."

But on Monday morning, I couldn't lift my arm.

I talked to my agent, Tom Condon, who was also Joe Montana's agent. Tom told me about an herbalist who helped Joe heal once when he was injured. Willing to try anything, I flew that same herbalist to my home on Tuesday. He immediately went to work in my kitchen, boiling a concoction that smelled like death. I don't know what all was in it, although I do recall him mentioning something about deer tendons. When the remedy was ready, I reluctantly gulped down a couple tall glasses of it. After giving it time to work its magic, we went outside to toss a football—and would you believe I was firing spirals with no pain? I told the herbalist he'd make millions if he bottled this stuff and sold it. I paid him and sent him home, feeling I'd made one of the best investments of my career.

Until Wednesday morning.

I woke up, made a mad dash for the bathroom, and threw it all up. Every drop. The only thing more disgusting than drinking deer tendon juice is vomiting deer tendon juice after it's been churning in your body for a day. What worked for Joe Montana clearly wasn't compatible with my system. And that wasn't all. I suddenly couldn't lift my arm again. I'd never felt so physically miserable.

My backup, Steve Walsh, a graduate of the University of Miami, was in his sixth season in the NFL. In week four, he led us to victory on the road against the New York Jets. He remained the starting quarterback and won the next two weeks at home against the Bills and Saints. His stats weren't great, but he got the job done.

Following our bye in week seven, and with my arm feeling better after rest and rehab with the team's training staff, I started against the Lions in Detroit. I passed for 309 yards and two touchdowns against my former team, but I also threw three interceptions. We lost 21–16. I got the start a week later on Monday night in Green

Bay, but I passed for just 34 yards and threw two interceptions before Dave Wannstedt pulled me. The Packers destroyed us in front of a national television audience, making me 1–4 as the starter, while Steve was 3–0. Feeling pressure from fans and some of his assistants, Dave told me the next morning that Steve would start the rest of the way.

And that was that.

An early season injury, four losses in a row as the starter, and an embarrassing demotion. I was still being paid a huge salary but no longer earning it, and the Chicago faithful were questioning why the Bears had signed me. It was the most significant letdown of my career, and it all occurred within the first eight weeks of the season. I felt like I'd been tossed into Lake Michigan with my hands tied behind my back and boulders strapped to my legs. I was sunk.

Depression had been trying to pry into my life for years. Now, it was crying with jubilation, "Yes! Finally! I'm in!"

CHAPTER 13

DEPRESSION AND A MOTHER'S LOVE

I really can't pinpoint the exact moment when depression first consumed me. It happened sometime at home the first day or two after the Bears benched me and I realized my only escape from my crumbling marriage was in ruins. But there was no denying it once it took over.

The American Psychiatric Association defines depression as "a common and serious medical illness that negatively affects how you feel, the way you think, and how you act. It can lead to a variety of emotional and physical problems and can decrease your ability to function at work and at home." Some of the many symptoms include sadness, loss of interest in activities once enjoyed, changes in appetite, increased fatigue, feelings of worthlessness, and suicidal thoughts.

My depression was like a gray, heavy fog that swiftly and continually rolled in until it was too dense to see through. Forming a basic thought was painful and paralyzing. Confusing and conflicting emotions overpowered all aspects of my life, even trivial ones. Nights were sleepless. Sunrises were hell. Food was tasteless; I had to force myself to eat. I didn't want to practice or be at home—I didn't want to be anywhere. Every sound was piercing, even laughter, but silence caused me to overthink. If I wasn't sad or irritated, I was disinterested. Happiness eluded me. Before my depression, I loved seeing people. I looked them in the eyes when we talked. But while in the throes of my depression, I tried to avoid everyone and certainly didn't make eye contact—I thought it was an invitation for them to say hello and initiate a conversation that I didn't want to have.

Nothing felt adequate anymore. My marriage never did, but at this point, I was also discounting my abilities as a father, especially after Griffen's tenuous start to life. It was an unjust assessment, but self-doubt rules every thought when you're mired in depression. I questioned my career and my capability to continue playing. *My shoulder is healed, but will there be a lasting impact? Will I be able to effectively throw a ball again? My last start against the Lions suggested that I might not. Even if I can, will the Bears still want me? Will any team? What will I do with the rest of my life if I'm a washed-up player at the age of thirty?* Instead of seeing the world and my life with a floodlight, I could only see them with a narrow laser beam that was fixed on the pain, sadness, and suffering. I lost my ability to see the big picture, alternatives to my problems, and any hope for a better tomorrow.

I'd become a prime example of how easy it is for a person to plunge from the highest of highs to the lowest of lows, how money and fame do not equal happiness, and how the life someone may appear to be living is not always what it seems.

Suicide first crossed my mind in late 1994, but it wasn't nearly as bad as it would be in 2015. At this point, I didn't plan anything or think about the details, like how or when. But when you're in a hole that dark and deep, it's almost inevitable that such thoughts will surface. The torment was too much. I simply didn't want to exist anymore.

Dr. Wildenhaus has always said that suicide is a permanent solution to what may be a temporary problem. He's right. But believing that is difficult when you're in the midst of depression, especially for the first time but even for the tenth time. Depression will do all it can to prevent any hope from creeping in. The negative thoughts and feelings don't rest. And how does one define *temporary* to a depressed person? A week? A month? A year? In many cases, a week feels like a month and a month can feel like a year because depression has no clock. Even if I want to believe you when you say I will eventually see the light at the end of the tunnel, you're saying it while I'm trapped in a deep, dark abyss and feel like I'm the only one on the planet experiencing it with no way of clawing myself out. When I'm in such a state, my brain won't grant me the serenity to be patient or trust your assessment.

In retrospect, misperceptions fueled my depression. I believe that's the case for many who suffer from the disease. Misperceptions—irrational, manufactured thoughts with little or no basis in truth that force us to isolate and doubt ourselves and everyone around us—are depression's fiercest weapons. My mindset was that if I wasn't fulfilling my expectations for myself—which I never felt I was when I was depressed—then everyone else must be disappointed in me too. And I took *everything* anyone said as negative and personal. There was no room for interpretation or middle ground. It was always bad and never good.

For example, after a blowout loss in 1994, a teammate called a players' meeting in the locker room to let guys air their grievances. One player stood up and made comments that I was sure were directed at me, even though he never looked at me or said my name. Reflecting on that incident now, I guarantee I was the furthest person from his mind. In fact, this meeting occurred after my demotion, so I wasn't even playing at the time. But because of my mental state, I was sure I was his target and loathed him for it. That only fueled my rage and made me question other players' comments during the meeting, which, in turn, created more irrational thoughts in my head.

I eventually sought professional help later that season. I wish I knew what made me do it or whom I reached out to, but that memory has been erased. I'd always assumed it was Dr. Wildenhaus because I thought he was the only professional I'd confided in until then, but he told me recently that after I went to the Bears, we didn't talk until 1995. I know I got help, though, because I began taking antidepressants in 1994, and someone prescribed them to me. Whoever was responsible, I'm eternally grateful because it was a vital first step in my healing journey.

Antidepressants weren't a cure-all, and they didn't work instantaneously, but over time, taking them helped temporarily level the playing field in my head. They eliminated some of the misperceptions in my mind and cleared some space so I could figure things out. They enabled me to process information better, avoid jumping to conclusions, and consider other points of view or possibilities. What I didn't like about antidepressants is that they felt artificial. As someone who's worked hard for everything he's achieved in life, taking medication to fix my mind didn't seem authentic. Yet I knew if I stopped, I would regress. My experience was that on an A to F grading scale, with no depression being an A and deep depression being an F, the antidepressants boosted me from an F to a constant C. It was far from perfect, but it was definitely an improvement, and one that gave me hope.

Surprisingly, my mom's presence was another significant piece of the puzzle that fit into my mental healing that season. She called me in late October and sensed my despair. I don't know how because I'm sure I didn't disclose my true feelings. Mustering the strength to exhibit a cheerful disposition and suppress emotions is old hat for people who are depressed. It's one reason why when a depressed person tries to inflict self-harm, most people are shocked when they hear about it. "I had no idea," they'll say. But Mom noticed, and she wanted to do something to help.

"Erik, how about I fly out to Chicago and spend some time with you," she offered.

"Mom, you don't have to do that. I'm fine," I lied.

"No, let me do this," she insisted. "I can take care of Griffen and give you and Marshawn a little break."

I relented, and when she arrived, I felt better immediately. I wasn't cured by any means, but she gave me a chance to breathe. She was like an antidepressant but more effective. She was my mom, and like most mothers, she was graced with a potent remedy: unconditional love. That was a side to her I'd rarely seen. That natural, nurturing maternal component she'd lacked when I was a kid had finally materialized. Maybe it was a result of her divorce from my dad or because she'd remarried a few years earlier. Or perhaps she could relate better to Kelley and me as adults. I don't know. But she was definitely a different person who treated me with the love and affection I'd always longed for from her.

She stayed for about a week and cleaned, cooked, and helped with Griffen. She didn't do or say anything specifically about my depression, but she didn't need to—her presence spoke volumes. Despite having a husband and a full-time job back in Southern California, she prioritized my well-being and put her life on hold to fly across the country. I still felt awful and found it difficult to get out of bed in the morning, but knowing she was there made life more tolerable. Even when she left, I knew she cared and was in my corner.

Those with depression often say they don't need people to offer magic words or solutions. They simply need them to be there, listen, and love. Amen to that.

Steve Walsh filled in nicely for me all year, much as I had for Rodney in Detroit when he was injured in 1991. Steve finished the 1994 season with an 8–3 record as the starter and an impressive wild card playoff win against the Vikings on the road. We lost in the divisional round to the 49ers, the eventual Super Bowl champions.

I assumed the Bears would trade me before the season started, or I would enter 1995 as Steve's backup. Neither was ideal. I loved Chicago and still wanted to be *the* guy they had expected me to be.

About a week before spring practice began in March 1995, Dave Wannstedt called me into his office. I was about to find out my fate.

CHAPTER 14

THE FLIP OF A SWITCH

Dave Wannstedt was succinct. Our meeting lasted no more than a minute.

"Erik, we brought you here for a reason, but you had some bad luck last year with the injury," he said, "so we're wiping the slate clean. You and Steve will get equal reps in practice, and the best man will be our starting quarterback."

Boom! I knew the job would be mine again. I wasn't being smug, just confident. Deep down, I felt that I was the better quarterback. That's why they signed me. I was also entering 1995 with a significant mental edge that I'd acquired in 1994.

You might be wondering how one acquires a mental edge while suffering from depression. Let me explain.

I struggled in the first three games before the injury because I wasn't up to par on our offensive scheme. It wasn't for lack of studying or effort; I simply didn't grasp it well enough or fast enough in training camp because it was nothing like the offense we ran in Detroit. But in those few hours of work each day during my depression—when I had to force myself to attend practices or games, grudgingly stand on the sidelines next to the coaches, and pretend like I cared—I naturally soaked in the intricacies of the offense. I learned the strategies behind the play calls, how to recognize blitzes, and when to call audibles. I watched how well receivers ran routes, our linemen's blocking techniques, and how quickly our running backs hit the holes. I could see what worked and didn't work for Steve and visualized myself in every situation he faced—without enduring a physical pounding. Steve did some things well and found ways to cobble wins together, but the offense averaged less than seventeen points per game in 1994, and I think the coaches and fans were anxious for something more. I knew I could provide it—and I did.

I started every game in 1995, delivering the best season of my life and one of the best ever for a Bears' quarterback. I passed for a franchise record of 3,838 yards and twenty-nine touchdowns. I threw just ten interceptions and had the NFL's fourth-highest passer rating. We averaged nearly twenty-five points a contest and scored the eighth-most points in the league. We finished the season 9–7, taking third place in our division, and tied the Falcons for the last wild card spot. Unfortunately, the Falcons won the tiebreaker by virtue of having a better record against the opponents we had in common. I had some great games and a couple I'd rather forget, but I put us into a position to win in the fourth quarter in fifteen of our sixteen matchups. Our division and conference were tough, though. One more win could've elevated us to the fourth seed in the playoffs. It was disappointing, but we had hope going into 1996.

In 1995, I became the quarterback the Bears expected me to be.

(Photo courtesy: Rich Kane Photography/Alamy Stock Photo)

During the 1995 season and the first couple months of the offseason, I learned two invaluable lessons about my depression: 1) it could flip on and off like a switch, and 2) I didn't control the switch. I've generally been referring to it as "my depression" because the illness differs for everyone. For some, that switch is more like a dimmer. For those people, when they go from depressed to not depressed, they may still feel the lingering effects and realize it could pounce again at any time. When they go from not depressed to depressed, they might still see a glimmer of hope. But for me, it was all or nothing. Dr. Wildenhaus explains the "all" phase well:

"It can certainly turn on a dime for some, and you were like that, Erik," he said. "For people who haven't experienced it, they can only imagine how frightening it can be to suddenly feel you've lost complete control over a situation or your life. It can be like a combat veteran or police officer who has PTSD and is triggered when they hear a firecracker on the Fourth of July—except in the case of depression, you may not even know what that trigger is. It's like walking down a street and falling into a manhole missing its cover. You don't see it coming and instantly find yourself in a black hole."

And when it was "nothing" for me, it really was nothing. As briskly and brutally as depression knocked me out in 1994, it vanished without a trace in 1995, and I found myself in a good place for several reasons.

One was that I reclaimed the starting role and was living up to my end of the contract. Football was enjoyable again. I was healthy. My confidence was back. That was how I'd envisioned my time in Chicago, and now I was living that vision.

Dr. Wildenhaus's presence in my life was another reason. Although he was still in Michigan, we talked by phone weekly. Then, when we realized the benefits of our phone conversations, he sent me cassette tapes recorded in his voice. They contained meditations and visualizations (often featuring background music by Eric Clapton, one of my favorite musicians) to help me relax in my hotel room on the night before a game or on the field during pregame warm-ups. I also flew Dr. Wildenhaus to Chicago on occasion to watch me play. He was gracious with his time, and the combination of these methods of staying in contact with him was instrumental in my accomplishments.

I also tapped into my spiritual side, something I'd never tried but thought could be another useful tool for sustaining my mental health. I wasn't brought up in a church or introduced to religion at home, but I learned about God in high school at Valley Christian and St. Genevieve. When I played with the Lions and Bears, whenever I heard my teammates talk openly about their faith, I was intrigued. I didn't turn to the Bible but to books such as C. S. Lewis's *Mere Christianity* to better my life. It helped me maintain perspective, relax, and prepare for whatever I needed to do next without feeling overwhelmed or distracted. I learned that believing in something greater than ourselves by setting aside our egos and the idea that we're in control of everything can go a long way toward a healthy mind and overcoming adversity.

Having that mindset also meant not getting caught up in the hype of being a professional athlete. Sure, I enjoyed some preferential treatment, like getting a table in a crowded restaurant if an employee there recognized me. But I avoided reading the papers and listening to talk radio. Not only did I not want my head to swell but I didn't want to feel any added pressure, especially being in the same town as the Bulls. The Bulls had already won three NBA championships and were on their way to winning three more. When fans get used to winning, they can become spoiled and expect the same from all their teams. Using the tightrope analogy, paying attention to any of that could've caused me to look down as the rope was raised higher. The less I knew what anybody was saying, the better.

After the season, I got away from football for about six weeks to spend time with Marshawn and Griffen, and all seemed good. But just before spring practice began in February 1996, the switch abruptly flipped, and I hit rock bottom again. I should've been pumped up for the new season after such a memorable one. I'd mastered our offense. My body was strong. And if I could put together a good year in 1996, the last of my contract, the Bears might make me another lucrative offer.

But depression swooped in—swift, hard, and unannounced. I wish I could say why, but I can't. Depression doesn't necessarily offer a motive. It does what it wants when it wants. I was at its mercy, wrapped in its grip for the second time in a year and a half, and I had to live with it until the switch flipped again. I continued talking to Dr. Wildenhaus and taking antidepressants, and those remedies helped enough that I don't recall having thoughts of suicide like I did in the fall of 1994. But once again, I was submerged in darkness.

The spring practices, training camp, and slate of preseason games were excruciating as I mustered every ounce of energy to play, talk to the media, and fake my happiness. We opened the regular season against Dallas on a Monday night and won, 22–6, despite my performance. I completed 12 of 27 passes for a paltry 133 yards and an interception. I performed no better the following two weeks in losses to the Redskins and Vikings. Based on a complex NFL calculation using four metrics, my passer ratings—on a scale of 0 to 158.3—were an embarrassing 44.2, 57.0, and 37.4, respectively. I had never strung together three such horrendous games at any level.

If you're a Bears' fan and wondered why I was so lousy after putting up such noteworthy numbers the year before, now you know. It was the first time I'd ever played with full-blown depression.

A week later, in a loss at Detroit, I snapped my neck trying to make a tackle after a turnover. I played through the pain but couldn't lift my throwing arm when the game was over. When we returned home, an MRI revealed two herniated discs that controlled my upper right chest, outside triceps, and the back of my shoulder. The team doctor told me that my season—and possibly my career—was finished.

CHAPTER 15

THE END OF AN ERA

I felt guilty about my 1996 season ending prematurely. Like I had in 1994, I thought I'd failed the fans and wasn't honoring my contract. But that feeling was short-lived this time. Depression caused me to play the worst football of my life, so I knew it would be best for the team and for me not to play for that reason alone. Of course, I never would've admitted that had I not been physically injured. It wasn't in my blood to quit. Also, there was—and still is—a considerable stigma attached to mental illness that I didn't want associated with me.

In the 1990s and prior, fans, media, and even coaches showed little mercy toward athletes regarding certain injuries. Unless a bone was broken—and even sometimes then—players were expected to suck it up and continue playing. I recall the anger Bulls fans directed at Scottie Pippen in 1990 when he sat out with a migraine in game seven of the Eastern Conference Finals against the Pistons. When asked about it by a *Tribune* reporter a year later, as the Bulls were on the verge of winning their first championship, Scottie said, "I don't think it ever will be forgotten. Even if we win the championship, I can see people still saying, 'If Pippen had played a year ago, they could have had two championships.' I think it's always going to be there."

He was right.

They won six championships in the next eight years, yet more than three decades later, people still criticize Scottie for the migraine. I realize that a migraine isn't "mental" in the way we generally discuss mental health. The physical effects of the headache—pulsating pain and double vision—are what sidelined him. But because it was associated with his brain and not an injury in the traditional sense, fans were ruthless. They called Scottie "soft" and questioned whether he could manage the pressure. Had he broken an arm or even severely sprained an ankle—something people could see that occurred while playing—he would've been vindicated.

Imagine the reaction from Chicago fans, six years after Scottie's migraine, if I'd removed myself as the Bears' quarterback because I was depressed. I likely would've been run out of town.

Since then, Americans have made significant strides in mental health awareness. When Simone Biles withdrew from the women's team gymnastics final at the 2020 Olympics for mental health reasons, she received a lot of fan and media support—much more than I would have twenty-four years earlier. But those who still don't understand that a mental injury can be as bad or worse than a physical one heavily criticized her. Yes, sometimes you have to fight through pain. I've done it on plenty of occasions. But at times, you know you can't, and it's admirable when you dare to acknowledge it and seek the help you need. I didn't have that courage in 1996. Few of us with depression did back then. Today, with widespread education and empathy, especially in schools where we can reach millions at a young age, we can continue to reduce that stigma.

As for treating my herniated discs, the doctor initially presented two options: fuse the vertebrae or take three epidural injections. I chose the latter because the former would've meant an immediate end to my career. But, unfortunately, my body didn't respond to the injections, so he proposed one more idea: drink a potion made of deer tendons.

Just kidding. Never again.

No, the last hope was to do nothing and trust that, with time, the discs would slide back into place. With nothing to lose, I did very little physical activity for the rest of the 1996 season—and it worked. By January 1997, I was pain-free and cleared to play. As a result, the Bears signed me to a one-year deal.

I was 4–9 in thirteen starts that season, and we finished 4–12 overall. I showed flashes of brilliance, mediocrity, and futility, sometimes in the same game. I passed for 3,011 yards, completed 58 percent of my throws, and tossed fourteen touchdowns and fourteen interceptions.

As rough as the season was, I enjoyed playing because I did so without any hint of depression; the switch had flipped within weeks after the start of spring practice.

Why? I have no idea. My marriage was still in shambles, and in some respects, at its worst. My body had become more susceptible to injury, reminding me that my career was nearing its end. And our team was one of the worst in the league. These were all good reasons for depression to hang around, but it didn't.

Remarkably, I wouldn't experience another bout of depression until the spring of 2015—three and a half years after Griffen died.

As I stated earlier, you need to know my background to understand what led me to the Good Nite Inn on August 18, 2015. But from 1997 until 2011, there isn't much worth noting. To stay on topic and return you to the hotel room sooner rather than later, I'll cut to the chase.

Following that dismal 1997 season, the Bears signed me to another one-year deal. I think they believed I had fuel left in the tank and would serve as a solid placeholder for their future quarterback. Several top-tier quarterbacks would be available in the 1999 draft, including Tim Couch from Kentucky, Donovan McNabb from Syracuse, and Cade McNown from UCLA. I figured the Bears were probably hoping to snag one of them.

In June 1998, about six weeks before the start of training camp, Dillon was born. Marshawn and I had been trying to have another baby, so unlike Griffen, Dillon's conception was not a shock. But his birth was.

In early June, with Dillon's due date about four weeks away and our family spending the off-season in Southern California, I was offered two courtside seats for game four of the NBA Finals in Chicago between the Bulls and the Utah Jazz. I thought it would be cool to take Griffen, who was about to turn five. After clearing it with Marshawn—who was thrilled to have some alone time before our second child arrived—Griffen and I flew to Chicago for the game on June 10. But just before tip-off that evening, Marshawn went into labor. We tried to catch a flight home immediately, but everything was booked out of both Chicago airports. We were stuck until the next morning. So, instead of being at the hospital for my son's birth, Griffen and I were at the game. I had my cell phone attached to my ear, receiving updates from the hospital the entire time.

There's an old saying: "People make plans, and God laughs." That's how I choose to explain Dillon being born a month early and hours after Griffen and I landed two thousand miles away with no way to get back. I was sad that I wasn't present for Dillon's arrival. At the same time, given that it was out of my hands, I was happy to have such a lasting memory with Griffen as the Bulls pulled off an 86–82 victory to take a 3–1 lead in the series.

I returned to Chicago a month later for training camp and earned the starting job. We lost our first four games before winning three of our next four. I injured my shoulder during that winning stretch and played hurt in victories against the Cowboys and the Tennessee Oilers (who had yet to be renamed the Titans). We entered the bye week at 3–5, and I was statistically on track for my best season since 1995—until tests on my shoulder revealed a

Griffen and me at game four between the Bulls and Jazz in 1998.
(Photo courtesy: Erik Kramer)

strained rotator cuff and a possible tear. We had been on
a roll and had a shot at the playoffs, but doctors said my
shoulder would worsen each game. The chances of me
making it through the season were almost zero. I needed
to shut down and have surgery, which was a severe blow
to the team. We lost seven of our last eight games and
finished 4–12 again.

After the season, the team owners fired Dave Wann-
stedt, his staff, and the general manager. Four months
later, in April 1999, the Bears drafted Cade McNown.
Before training camp that summer, new head coach Dick
Jauron had me work out to ensure my arm was okay.
After proving it was and receiving clearance from doc-

tors, Dick called me into his office. I assumed he wanted to discuss my role in relation to Cade.

"Erik," Dick said, "I'm sorry to tell you we're letting you go."

What?

He explained that they didn't want any incumbrances for Cade, although I didn't see myself as one. I knew they expected Cade to be the future. He was a highly touted rookie and twelve years younger than me. Even so, he could've learned from my success. Instead, the Bears brought in Shane Matthews to fill my role. Shane, who'd been a backup with the Bears for a few years, had only played a couple of games in 1996. Then he went to the Carolina Panthers for two years, where he didn't play at all. Ironically, Shane would still be playing for the Bears in 2001, while Cade's last NFL snap came in 2000.

The day after my release, San Diego signed me as Jim Harbaugh's backup. I started three games a few weeks into the 1999 season when Jim was injured, and we won two of them. Though Jim was healthy and ready to play for our week eight game in Kansas City, I started—but I didn't last long. Jim replaced me in the first quarter after I fumbled, threw an interception, and took a few hard hits. We lost, 34–0. I didn't think much of the hits, but a few days later, I woke up in the middle of the night with insufferable pain ricocheting through my arms, back, and neck. I was alone in a house that Marshawn and I had rented in Del Mar, about half an hour outside San Diego. She was with the boys, over three hours away, at our home in Oak Park, which is about fifteen miles north of Malibu.

Barely able to move, I rolled from the bed onto the floor, slid on my shoes, and snatched my keys from the nightstand. I crawled to the car, pausing every few seconds to let out a yelp and catch my breath. When I finally reached the vehicle, I climbed in from my knees and contorted my body to minimize the pain. Like a little old lady, I drove to the hospital with my head barely high enough to see over the steering wheel. Fortunately, given the late hour, I had most of the road to myself because I'm sure I crossed the center line several times. When I got to the emergency room, I was once again diagnosed with herniated discs. The doctor said one more hit on the gridiron could paralyze me.

Aside from the deaths I've faced, I have never cried much. But I did that night as the reality of my situation hit me. My emotions ran the gamut: relief that there would be no more weekly collisions with defensive linemen, fear about life after football, gratitude for the teams that had given me the opportunity to play in the NFL, disappointment for all my injuries, and pride for all I had accomplished. For a kid who didn't play quarterback much in high school, was initially ignored by colleges, went undrafted, crossed a picket line, spent more days in Canada bartending than playing football, and had to dial his way back into the NFL with a rotary phone, I did pretty well. Not a single season went as planned, but I did my best with what I could control and made the most of every chance I was given.

I loved sharing my career with my boys, as I did on this day at Soldier Field in Chicago. *(Photo courtesy: Erik Kramer)*

It took me a year to physically heal and return to normal, and the transition to retirement, surprisingly, was seamless. Griffen was eight and wanted to play football, so I coached his team (and Dillon's when he was old enough a few years later). I started a summer camp for high school quarterbacks. Former USC and Cleveland Browns' linebacker Clay Matthews Jr., who lived nearby and coached the freshman team at Agoura Hills High School, brought me on board as an assistant. And out of the blue, a guy from Fox Sports, who I'd met at one of my camps, asked if I'd be interested in broadcasting. I said yes even though I had no experience, but I caught on quickly. For the next ten years, I worked in various capacities at Fox Sports, including as a pro and college play-by-play analyst and as a studio analyst.

During this decade, Marshawn and I sold our home in Oak Park and bought one in Agoura Hills, but we separated multiple times. When we did—to make it as smooth and pleasant for the boys as possible—we rented an apartment in Oak Park. Each time, rather than one of us living in one location permanently, Marshawn and I swapped living quarters weekly. In other words, the boys never had to leave their Agoura Hills home. They were only with one parent at a time, but at least they had some stability.

And that's fourteen years in a nutshell. I'd dodged depression and pretty much naturally. I took antidepressants on occasion but nothing consistently. Football was still part of my life, just in a different way. And Marshawn was still part of my life in the same way. The most significant challenge during these years was raising Griffen. Nothing ever came easy for him, but Marshawn and I were determined to give him the best life we could, and he always managed to maneuver through difficult circumstances.

Until the last weekend in October 2011.

CHAPTER 16

THE DEATH OF MY SON

Griffen had a complex and grueling life from day one. The deadly bacteria that attacked him at birth was the first of many hardships. He couldn't sit still in school or at home. Reading was difficult. He lacked the patience to work through anything that didn't come easy, and very few things did. Plus, his unique disposition made it tough for him to create and maintain friendships. He began dabbling in marijuana late in middle school, likely as an escape from his reality. Griffen knew that he rarely fit into any situation or group but didn't understand why. Marshawn and I didn't either.

In 2007, the summer after Griffen finished eighth grade, we had him evaluated by a neuropsychologist, who found a severe defect in the frontal lobe of Griffen's brain. The doctor concluded that Griffen would always be limited in his ability to function around others in ways society demanded, which is what we had experienced to that point.

That same summer, on the recommendation of our family therapist, we took Griffen to the Second Nature therapeutic wilderness camp in Utah, a haven for struggling teens. I flew with Griffen to Salt Lake City, where two people from Second Nature met us at the airport to take him to the camp. I knew this experience could potentially provide Griffen with the structure and therapy he so desperately needed, and as his father, it energized me with hope. But any respite it provided was temporary.

I believe the most significant fallout of Griffen's condition was his inability to relate to his peers, especially in high school. He attended Oak Park High School for the first semester of his freshman year before transferring to Agoura High School, and he struggled at both. When he couldn't make the desired connections, he searched for others in less attractive circles. Some of the kids who finally accepted him were the ones who introduced him to the drugs that eventually killed him.

Griffen started dabbling with alcohol around ninth grade. At a birthday party we threw for him, he covertly served his friends drinks in the garage, unbeknownst to the adults who were there. That may sound tame for a high schooler, but I share it for two reasons. One is that it didn't faze Griffen to take such a risk with his parents in the house, even though he knew we would be angry and not tolerate it. The other is that Marshawn and I were unaware of most of Griffen's wrongdoings until he told us during therapy sessions. Marshawn and I accepted some blame for that, but teenagers are also good at hiding what they don't want their parents to know, no matter how much parents think they know.

Another example of Griffen taking a risk right under our noses also occurred during his freshman year. We had a large golden retriever and a doggie door in the laundry room that the dog used to get in and out of the house. One night, I was awoken when I heard some rustling coming from Griffen's room. I walked in to find eight teenagers. Griffen had told them they could sneak in through the doggie door after Marshawn and I went to bed. Even though he knew we disapproved of most of them being in the house because of their negative influence on him, he didn't understand why I was so upset. It was less about those kids being in the house and more about him skirting the rules to get what he wanted. If Griffen were staring at a ten-foot wall, he would figure out how to get over it without considering why the wall was there.

Griffen scored drugs from dealers at a local park and acquired alcohol by hanging outside a liquor store and paying someone of age to buy it. His dependency started with pot, beer, and liquor, then gravitated to Xanax bars, cough syrup, and other drugs until he discovered heroin. I've learned that's how it works with many heroin addicts. They don't jump right into it. They gradually experiment with other substances, each one a little more harmful than the previous one and acquired with more planning, until they reach that peak.

Around October of Griffen's sophomore year, Marshawn found an excellent mental health facility in Malibu called Visions Adolescent Treatment Center. Griffen had a dedicated counselor there, and we were heavily involved in the process through discussions and meetings. After three months of inpatient treatment, Griffen returned home and continued with Visions's outpatient therapy, which included a formal yet individualized education in lieu of returning to a traditional school. It lasted through the rest of his sophomore year and his entire junior year. The caring people there—including his counselor, his teacher, and several teacher's aides—had Griffen believing he could one day attend college and be successful. His time away from a traditional school and football removed him from unhealthy relationships and taught him healthy living habits. It seemed like he'd finally turned a corner.

Griffen returned to a traditional school for his senior year, choosing Thousand Oaks High School for a fresh start, and it was obvious from the outset that he was a kinder and happier person with more focus. During the early part of that football season, I'd occasionally meet him over his lunch period with a chessboard in the school parking lot. I would ask him to name a formation and play from the team's playbook and move the pieces on the board to demonstrate how it worked. It was fascinating to watch the wheels turn in his mind as he showed me with such confidence and clarity. On a shelf in my living room, I have a photo of Griffen and a bishop chess piece next to it to remind me of his transformation, along with how grateful he was to us for helping him get there.

"If it weren't for you and Mom, I'd be in jail or dead," he said to me one day. He knew he'd put himself in many precarious positions and was lucky to have survived. This new attitude gave us hope.

On Friday, October 28, 2011, I was driving Griffen to Marshawn's after one of his football games when he asked me if Coach Fenwick—my coach at Pierce, who by then was coaching at Los Angeles Valley College— might let him try out for football after graduation. I was floored. This was coming from a kid who never thought about anything beyond the current day—or minute. I told Griffen I was sure Coach Fenwick would welcome him. This led to an honest, thoughtful, and delightful discussion about his future. And I was particularly thankful that he'd initiated it.

Never in my wildest dreams—or nightmares—did I think it would be the last conversation we would ever have.

Around midmorning on Sunday, October 30, I received a call from the Lost Hills Sheriff's Station.

"Mr. Kramer," the deputy said. "I need you to come down here."

"What for?" I asked.

"With all due respect, sir," he replied, "it would be best if you come down here immediately. I can explain when you arrive."

My heart fell into my stomach.

I knew.

The police had called me before when Griffen got into trouble, but they always told me why they were calling. I knew there was only one thing so awful that it couldn't be said over the phone—something I didn't want to see or hear.

My premonition was confirmed when I pulled in and saw the officer waiting for me outside.

"Mr. Kramer," he said somberly. "I am so sorry to tell you that your son Griffen was found dead this morning."

I don't remember anything else either of us said or how I reacted. The next thing I recall is riding in a squad car in silence to the house where Griffen's body was. The shock had already set in. Each time Griffen had been in trouble, I always thought the same thing: *At least he's still alive.* This time, I was grappling with the realization that I couldn't say that anymore. His time had expired, and there was nothing I could do to bring him back.

When we walked into the home, the owner was sitting at the kitchen table. I recognized her from Al-Anon, a support group for people—many of them parents—affected by those who are addicted to alcohol or drugs. After exchanging solemn greetings, her son walked in. Without prompting or any introduction, he told me he had nothing to do with Griffen's death.

"We were just hanging out," he said. "I don't know what happened."

Neither did I. I didn't remember ever meeting this kid. He only seemed concerned about exonerating himself. I didn't even know yet how my son had died, when he died, or where his body was. And this was his greeting? I said nothing to him.

Eventually, Chris Germann, the man I would text nearly four years later from my hotel room, came in. He was one of the officers working that day. We all sat at the table where hardly a word was spoken, at least by me. After several minutes, another officer told me to follow him. He wanted me to identify Griffen's body, and I thought seeing him might bring me closure, if there is such a thing. But I don't think there ever is when you lose someone so tragically, especially a child. The "what ifs" never stop. The guilt never completely goes away. Time can heal wounds, but the scars are always there.

We walked into a bedroom where Griffen was faceup on the floor. My chest tightened as I tried to control my breathing.

"We can leave now," the officer said.

"No, I'm okay," I assured him.

I wasn't. How could I be?

Around this time, my longtime friend Robert "Espo" Espinoza got word from his son about what had happened. His son and Griffen used to hang out together. Espo later told me about that moment from his perspective:

"I raced to your house, and a few cops were outside," Espo said. "They gave me the address where I could find you, so I headed straight over there. When I pulled up, Marshawn was out front pacing along the sidewalk. She was in denial and kept saying there was no way it could be Griffen, but she couldn't bring herself to go inside. She asked me if I would go in, so I did.

"When I got to the room where Griffen's body was, you were kneeling at Griffen's head, holding his hand, and crying," Espo continued. "I knelt next to you and cried with you. There wasn't anything else I could do. Nothing I could say. It was heart-wrenching to witness. I couldn't imagine what you were going through."

When your child is lying dead in front of you—I can't compare it to anything. The pain cuts deep into your soul. Sadness washes over you. That image of him remains emblazoned on my mind to this day, and the only comfort it gives me is how peaceful Griffen looked. Never had I seen him so calm, so free of pain, so free of demons. There'd be no more battles between good and evil, no more worries about acceptance or rejection, no more internal or external conflicts of any kind.

Just peace.

I rode back to the police station in the same squad car and called the father of Dillon's friend Michael. Dillon had spent the night at their house. I told Michael's father what had transpired and asked him if he could bring Dillon home, and I would meet them there.

Dillon recalls the morning vividly and recently shared his memory of it with me:

"Michael's dad woke us up and took Michael out of the room," Dillon said. "Then they came back in together and said they needed to take me home. They didn't say why or show any panic, but I could tell something was wrong. After the short drive home, you were waiting for me outside. You looked disheveled, like you hadn't slept in days. Inside, I noticed two chairs were out of place. You'd positioned them for us to sit down and talk. I'm thinking, 'Am I in trouble for something? Did I not turn in my homework?' Then your eyes got moist and your voice cracked. I knew it was something much bigger. Grandma had been sick with cancer, so I thought maybe she'd died. But you said it was Griffen. I didn't believe you at first. I figured I'd heard you wrong. Or you'd said it wrong. I'd just seen Griffen the night before. I thought, *This can't be happening.* When you convinced me it was true, I started screaming."

Learning about Griffen's death was the most painful moment of my life. Having to tell Dillon was a close second. At the tender age of thirteen, he'd lost his one and only brother and, in many respects, his hero.

"Griffen was five years older than me, but we had a lot of fun together when we were little," Dillon recalled. "We were very competitive. I learned a lot from him, like how to play ball and how to stuff things in your pillow during a pillow fight before whacking the other person. He would pick on me like big brothers do, and I would instigate stuff and pretend to be innocent like every little brother. I think he resented me as we got older because I'd tag along with him and his friends. Then I got my own friends and didn't want to tag along. There was definitely a growing separation between us. But then our chance encounter the night before he died—that was really awesome."

The encounter Dillon is referring to took place at a youth football complex up the road from Michael's house. Griffen and Dillon were both watching some games, each was with his own friends. I was there too, by myself. Dillon and his friends were tossing a football near the bleachers in the end zone when the ball got away and rolled toward Griffen. Rather than ignoring it or kicking the ball away, as he once would've done, Griffen scooped it up and played catch with them. Eventually, Dillon's friends ran off to play somewhere else, leaving Griffen and Dillon playing catch. These two brothers loved each other and generally got along but couldn't always connect, mainly because of Griffen's struggles. Since he'd come out of therapy, Griffen had been looking out more for Dillon. And as Griffen changed for the better, so did their relationship. Neither of them noticed me watching

Dillon and Griffen with our dog, Oso. *(Photo courtesy: Erik Kramer)*

them that night, but I couldn't have scripted this simple and spontaneous moment between my sons any better.

I would later learn that it had the same effect on Dillon.

"My friends and I were playing two-hand touch when, all of a sudden, Griffen walked out to join us," Dillon said. "I thought, *What the hell is this?* Then I pushed the envelope by giving him a big hug, and he hugged me back. That was huge for him to do in front of other people. And he wasn't high. He was finally comfortable in his own skin and not afraid to show it. Then all of my friends dispersed, and it was just Griffen and me playing catch and having a deep conversation. He gave me a 'take life by the horns' kind of speech, telling me to stay away from all the crap he'd gotten into and that I was good at school and should lean on that.

"When his friend told him they had to leave, Griffen threw me the ball, gave me the peace sign, and left," Dillon continued. "That's the last time I ever saw him."

Memories like that have helped me come to terms with Griffen's death, at least to the extent that a father can reconcile something so catastrophic. I know I poured all my love into my sons the best I knew how. I wasn't the perfect father, but I tried to teach Griffen right from wrong and to have respect for himself and others. I coached his teams. I helped get him into the best treatment programs available. I immersed myself in his therapy and never gave up on him. I tried to have the type of relationship with him that my parents struggled

Griffen's gravesite. *(Photo courtesy: Erik Kramer)*

to have with me. And for a kid diagnosed with a brain that would never jive with society's norms, the conversation we'd had in the car about his future and the one he had with Dillon while tossing the football showed he was finally finding his way.

But Griffen made one fatal mistake beyond my control or knowledge that erased all that headway: he returned to the wrong crowd. We all need connections to survive at various stages in our lives. Nobody can navigate life on their own. But associating with people who don't enrich us can create stagnation. And worse, they can steer us down destructive paths that can lead to insurmountable ruin.

I've asked myself how Dillon was born to and raised by the same parents yet hasn't had the troubles Griffen had. I believe the primary reason is that Dillon didn't have Griffen's brain condition.

"I would also say that one of the best parts of being a younger brother is learning from the mistakes the older brother made," Dillon told me. "I learned from his experiences, good and bad."

And I would add that Dillon has kept good company throughout his life. The kids Griffen connected with—those he settled for when nobody else would accept him—had little value or respect for life. At least not for Griffen's life. And they proved that the night he died.

As investigators later determined and told me, Griffen and two other boys met in a park in Agoura Hills on Saturday night, then drove to a nearby street, where Griffen injected himself with heroin. After Griffen overdosed and lost consciousness, one of the boys—the one who told me in his mother's kitchen that he didn't know what had happened—took Griffen home and left him there rather than getting him medical attention. That boy then allegedly went to another party while Griffen died alone in the room where I would identify his body.

While I didn't read or watch any media coverage of Griffen's story, I've recently found a couple of archived articles online from the *Thousand Oaks Acorn* that explain the aftermath of Griffen's death. Three weeks after Griffen died, the paper stated that the Los Angeles County Sheriff's Department had raided six homes as a result of information they'd received while investigating Griffen's death. They seized forty-eight pieces of evidence, including heroin, cocaine, and marijuana. Child Protective Services took six children from those homes into custody because of their living conditions. And three teenagers, including the one who took my son back to his house, were charged with involuntary manslaughter for Griffen's death.

The most alarming piece of information in the article—even more than the fact that three teens had been charged—was that six children had been removed from their homes. Think about the hell Child Protective Services must have walked into to determine it best to take those kids away. That's when I realized that as massive as the hole was in my heart from losing my son, he was just a number when it comes to the sheer volume of victims of the drug epidemic. It's easy for someone to say that Griffen died in vain. But maybe he didn't if his death means those six children get a chance at a better life.

A year later, the *Acorn* reported that the boy who took Griffen home had been held legally responsible for his death. He pleaded no contest to involuntary manslaughter and received five years' probation and ninety days of community labor. I don't know if anything happened to the other two teens. While Griffen was undoubtedly accountable for what he did to himself, medical experts agreed that he could've recovered if someone had taken him to a hospital or called for immediate help.

"I think Griffen bears some responsibility for his lifestyle and the company he kept," I told the *Acorn* after the sentencing. "The gist of what I feel about this situation is that (the boy who pleaded no contest) was just incapable—not criminal—but incapable of doing the right thing.

He'll have to live with that and make some changes in his life if he hopes to live a good life."

I also told the paper that I'd forgiven the boy. But I didn't do it for him. I did it for me.

"What you don't forgive you carry around," I said. "I think it's good that it's come to a conclusion."

I don't know where he or the other two boys who were charged are today. I haven't searched for them, and I won't. My focus has been, and will continue to be, on moving forward. But I hope they've made positive changes and are living productive and peaceful lives. It would be the most responsible and honorable way to make amends for their roles in this tragedy.

CHAPTER 17

A FINAL GOODBYE

The public's response to Griffen's death was astounding. On Saturday, November 5, thousands of people packed Calvary Community Church in Westlake Village for his funeral. Their tears, laughter, and poignant recollections reinforced how remarkable Griffen was. I scanned the massive church in awe of the wall-to-wall crowd. *I wish Griffen could see this. Look at everyone who cared about him.* His death drained my heart, but witnessing his legacy that day refilled it.

The love continued to flow for the next two months. A steady stream of people visited to check on my well-being, drop off meals, or reminisce about Griffen, including friends, classmates, teammates, parents, coaches, teachers, and even a grieving father I'd never met who'd lost his daughter to heroin and wanted to share his story to help me with mine. The selfless compassion from all these people propelled me through the initial phase of grief. I was deeply grateful, especially considering several other strenuous events happening around the same time.

One was my divorce. Earlier that year, Marshawn had filed for it with my cooperation. Before Griffen died, we were working on resolving various issues, including where the boys would live. We'd been separated more often than not during the previous decade—sometimes for a year or two, and at this point, since March 2010—so I think we finally wore each other down and asked ourselves why we were continuing to do this to ourselves. Plus, by then, we were older and wiser, so as long as we focused on caring for our kids, it made sense to split for good. Divorce is never easy for a child at any age, but neither is living with the two people who brought you into this world when they don't get along, as I knew firsthand from my own childhood. The divorce became final in September 2012.

I may not be the best person to give advice on how to have a successful marriage, but one suggestion I can offer is to know yourself intimately before committing to a lifetime partner. When you know who you are, what you want, and what you're capable of, you'll be better equipped with the wisdom to make healthy decisions, avoid irreparable pitfalls, and grow in sync together throughout your married life.

Another significant event around this time was my mother's decline. Our relationship had been reborn when she flew to Chicago in 1994, during my first bout with depression. Over the next eighteen years, we connected better emotionally than we had in the previous thirty. We visited each other frequently, talked on the phone, and genuinely enjoyed each other's company.

My relationship with my mother grew with time. *(Photo courtesy: Erik Kramer)*

On Mother's Day 2011, Dillon and I golfed with Mom and her husband, Doug. When we finished, Doug took Dillon to their town house, while Mom and I stayed at the course for lunch.

"I haven't been feeling well lately," she confided. "I had some tests done last week and will get the results soon."

I was shocked. She'd always been a pillar of strength and a model of good health. She'd just played eighteen holes of golf with me and looked like she could play another eighteen.

"You don't need to worry about it," she assured me. "I'm going to be fine." The next day, her test results revealed that she had stage four uterine cancer.

Mom elected to have a complex and dangerous surgery a few weeks later, followed by intense chemotherapy. She came through it all pretty well, but just after

Griffen died, the cancer returned, and she spent the next several months in and out of the hospital. I kept her company and later told my Aunt Patrice that it was the most meaningful time I'd ever spent with my mom. The conversations were vast, genuine, and inspiring. There were no barriers between us anymore. The past was long gone, but we knew our time together was short. We had the present and seized the moment.

"Mom," I said to her one day, "do you feel you were loved in life?"

I asked because her upbringing was strict, her marriage to my dad was miserable, and I knew little about Doug. He and I were cordial but not particularly close. And even though I couldn't have done much if she answered no, I wanted her to die happy. I needed to know that she felt fulfilled—that she felt loved.

"Oh, of course," she said sincerely. "Look at the wonderful life I've had. So many people have been good to me." She didn't say much more and didn't have to. I heard what I wanted to hear.

Mom passed peacefully on July 8, 2012, less than nine months after Griffen died. Although she was relatively young at sixty-eight, there was a natural progression to her death due to her illness, which somehow made it easier to accept. But because it happened so soon after Griffen's sudden death, I recognized the growing void in my life. And it was compounded a few weeks later when my dad was diagnosed with incurable esophageal cancer.

Dad never stopped drifting. He moved from town to town, home to home, job to job. In 2010, he was living with a woman in Southern California and serving as a caretaker for her son while she was working. In return, she let Dad live with them rent-free. No, Dad wouldn't have been my first choice to fulfill such a role, but I noticed his demeanor had changed as he aged. Years earlier, when I'd invited him to be more involved in Griffen and Dillon's lives, I was impressed by how he interacted with them. He listened better and spoke more lovingly than he ever had with me. He wasn't just tolerable to be around, he was genuinely likable. He was grateful to have the opportunity to get to know his grandsons, and I was happy they got to know their grandfather.

Mom had even noticed that he'd changed. In 2010, when Mom and Doug hosted Thanksgiving, they invited several friends and relatives, including Kelley's family, my boys, me—and Dad. Mom welcomed him with Doug's blessing, and Dad accepted. It was an incredible act of graciousness on Mom's part and an unprecedented day for all of us. For the first and only time in my life, my parents, my sister, our children, and I broke bread around the same table. It was a joyous occasion and one of my last and best memories of our entire family together.

Dad's health never improved. The cancer was unrelenting and debilitated him for three insufferable years. He passed away in September 2015, two weeks after I'd tried to kill myself. Fortunately, given his condition, he died not knowing what I'd done.

Our family's Thanksgiving together. Dad is standing, second from the left. Mom is sitting on the far left. I'm standing on the right, while Griffen is sitting below me. Kelley is next to him, and Dillon is on the far right.

(Photo courtesy: Erik Kramer)

I did my best to make him comfortable during the three years he was ill. When I found him being tended to by nuns in a convent thirty minutes away, I moved him to an apartment near me to get him better medical care and to give the nuns a break. It allowed us to reestablish our relationship, like Mom and I had. My talks with him may not have been as personal, deep, or frequent as they were with Mom—that wasn't his way—but they drew us closer and gave us a better understanding of each other.

Since college, I had tried to emotionally disconnect myself from my dad because of his overbearing persona. And I thought I'd succeeded. But during his illness, I learned that I really hadn't. On his most difficult days, when the cancer wouldn't let him swallow food or speak with any strength, I was moved by his vulnerability. As a salesman, he could talk his way through anything. As a father, he was never short on giving advice. As a coach, he chatted up his players and kept the umpires and officials on their toes. Now, as I reflected on his life in its entirety, I saw him not just as my father or my mother's husband, but as the little boy whose mom had left him and dad had sent him away to live with someone else. That must've crushed his spirit, self-worth, and trust in others. What chance did he have to find purpose or passion in anything?

And yet, when I was born, he dedicated himself to me. His methods weren't always the best, and he lacked the self-awareness to learn from his mistakes. But as misdirected as his efforts often were, he tried. I think about

Dad and me. *(Photo courtesy: Erik Kramer)*

all the time he spent with me: the hundreds of practices and games he coached and his constant search for opportunities for me to play and succeed at the highest level. He believed in me when nobody else did—which means he also believed in himself and his ability to help me get there. Considering his upbringing, that's pretty remarkable.

I stated earlier that many of my better judgments as an adult have resulted from what I learned *not* to do from my parents. But I never thought about that from my dad's perspective. He didn't always know how to be a good father, but one thing he knew not to do was abandon his children. Even when he and Mom divorced, he was the one who took Kelley. Yes, he had his issues, and his flaws always seemed to be magnified, but I still loved him. I know that because of how painful it was to watch him suffer in the end.

CHAPTER 18

OUT OF OPTIONS

In April 2015, as Dad was living out his final few months, I was driving home from his place one afternoon when the depression switch flipped. It was irrefutable. Like a volcano that starts to bubble, I couldn't stop its surge. An explosion was imminent. It had been nearly nineteen years since I'd had that dreadful sensation. But unlike my previous bouts, something was different this time. I got the sense that the depression wasn't just trying to send me into a funk or make it difficult to get out of bed. This had a much rougher edge and a more serious agenda.

I usually didn't know precisely why depression emerged when it did, but this time was clear: I was on the verge of losing my father, who'd become terminally ill right after I'd lost my mother, who had died right after I'd lost my older son. I was also retired from broadcasting and had little to distract me, so the enormity of the losses was palpable. When the depression hit in the 1990s, I knew I had reasons to live. I didn't feel that way this time. Yes, I still had Dillon and loved him with everything I had, but he and I had gradually grown apart. It wasn't anything out of the ordinary, just a teenage son and his dad naturally butting heads, as many do. As a result, since the divorce, he'd been spending more time with his mom than he was with me, and he was doing well. That caused the depression to create the misperception in my mind that Dillon didn't need my baggage and would be better off without me. Parents unfamiliar with depression may not be able to fathom that. But while they're asking, "You love your son, yet you're going to leave him?" depression emphatically responds with, "You love your son, so you need to leave him!" You get two completely different meanings with that simple change in syntax, and yet both are valid, depending upon one's state of mind. That's the sovereignty depression has.

I'd gone to therapy for three years after Griffen's death. It had helped, so in 2014, the therapist and I had agreed that I didn't need to continue. So why not go back, you might wonder. That's how this version of depression was different. The moment it hit me in the car that day, I was psychologically transforming into the person you met in the first chapter. I wasn't thinking about how to help myself get out of this rut or survive each day; I was on a mission to remove myself from the equation. In my mind, the world didn't need me. I'd served my purpose and was no longer relevant. As I mentioned earlier, Dr. Wildenhaus says suicide is a permanent solution to what may be a temporary problem, and even though I knew that to be accurate, I couldn't convince myself of it in my current state. My perspective was skewed. Nothing was temporary about death—Griffen and my mom wouldn't be returning. The depression made that abundantly clear.

My thoughts didn't waver for the next several weeks as I scoured the Internet for ways to end my life. With numerous options, a bullet to the head was my method of choice. Quick, easy, and painless. Under the chin, like the warden in the movie *The Shawshank Redemption*.

In late May, I drove about twenty miles north to Simi Valley and bought a gun for the first time in my life: a Sig Sauer 9mm pistol. The salesman didn't ask why I wanted it or my experience level. I'd done my research and sounded pretty knowledgeable. After picking out the piece, I filled out the necessary paperwork. I could pick it up after the background check cleared around the third week in June.

A week or two after my purchase, my friend Lisa stopped by the house. We were sitting in the living room talking when I told her matter-of-factly about my depression and that suicide had crossed my mind. She was stunned by my candor.

"Have you felt this way before?" she asked.

"Yes, but it's been a long time. Not since I played football."

"Wait here a minute," she said.

Lisa went into the kitchen and dialed the National Suicide Prevention Lifeline. When a counselor answered, Lisa explained my situation to her.

"Talk to this person," Lisa said as she returned to the room and handed me the phone. "She can help you through this."

Lisa sat with me as I spent roughly twenty minutes answering the counselor's questions. I intentionally didn't say anything to signal to her that I was on the verge of harming myself, but Lisa was still concerned when we hung up, as my Aunt Patrice recalls:

"Lisa met with me the next day because she said she was worried about you," Patrice told me. "She wanted to know if you could stay with me until we found a facility where you could get help. Of course I said yes, but I wasn't sure how to handle it. I knew you'd dealt with depression years earlier during your football career, but I wasn't personally involved and had no experience with depression myself. While you stayed with me, you called your friend Eric (Hipple), who told you to fly out to Michigan. You and I discussed it, and you agreed to go. I thought, *This is perfect. He's going to get the help he needs.*"

Eric Hipple was the quarterback for the Lions throughout the 1980s. He retired the year before I signed. We got to know each other through our connections to the Lions, broadcasting, and, eventually, depression. His mother suffered from depression. He did, too, during high school and college, and he attempted suicide in 1997. His son died from suicide in 2000.

"The wheels came off for me when my son passed," Eric once shared with me. "I was numb for a whole year. I was self-medicating and knew I had to figure out what was going on."

In 2001, Eric checked himself into the University of Michigan Depression Center (now the Frances and

Kenneth Eisenberg and Family Depression Center), one of the best such facilities in the country. After being successfully treated, the organization hired him as a community outreach specialist in 2004. He continues to serve in that role today, focusing on suicide prevention and other mental health issues, particularly for military veterans and former NFL players.

Eric told me he would enroll me in the center's thirty-day program. I didn't expect it to help or change my mind, but since I hadn't set a timeline for my suicide—I still had personal affairs to tend to and wouldn't have my gun for a couple more weeks—I didn't see any harm in going. So I went. But I didn't buy in, as Eric recently told me:

"You were so flat when you got here," he said. "You kept to yourself in your room, and I couldn't motivate you to do much. You stayed for the entire thirty days and did a lot of what we asked, but I think you'd made up your mind before you even arrived that you were going to take your own life and weren't going to tell us."

Eric is right. I may have shown signs of depression, but I never let him think I was suicidal. Nor did I let on to Patrice, Dr. Wildenhaus, who visited me a couple times during those thirty days, or Dillon, whom I talked to about my trip before I left. The depression was firmly anchored and much too powerful to allow me to show my cards.

"Many people who commit suicide have three things in common," Eric told me. "The first is that life is so tough for them that they feel they're hindering other people's happiness. They feel sad and try to cope, but eventually, they think they're dragging everyone around them down and need to get out of their way.

"The second is that they have to have the ability to override self-preservation, which isn't easy to do. The brain is built for solving problems and is really good at it. But if they're depressed and nothing they try to get out of it makes them better, their brain will start to tell them and eventually convince them that they can't fix it. That's when they consider death as a solution.

"The third thing is that once they've made up their mind to do it, they stop sharing their troubles and keep their plan to themselves. They don't see a reason to tell anyone how they're feeling or to seek help because things are good to them. And 'good' means they feel they've finally found a solution, which is death."

All three of those points applied to me.

When I returned to California in late July, feeling no different than before I'd left for Michigan, I picked up my gun at the store and went to the shooting range. With the depression in complete control, I laughed as I fired at a target several feet away. *What am I doing here? I'll be shooting myself at point-blank range. This is a waste of time. I should be at home getting things ready.* By which, I was referring to more critical issues that needed my attention. In other words, getting my personal affairs in order.

I spent the rest of July and the first couple weeks of August writing letters, paying bills, and sifting through my finances. Anna and Kelley took their kids to Hawaii for a week during this time and begged me to go with them, but I had no interest. I lived in solitude, hunkering down in my house and talking to almost nobody. Except for some brief moments while writing the letters, none of this was emotional. I felt I was doing what I needed to do. The depression kept me calm and focused as I treated each day like any other—until I finally reached *the* day.

And that's how I ended up at the Good Nite Inn on Tuesday, August 18, 2015, when I finally pulled the trigger.

CHAPTER 19

REDUCED TO A CHILD

I should've watched *The Shawshank Redemption* again because the bullet shredded my tongue, ripped through my nasal cavity, gouged out a chunk of my brain, exited through the top of my skull—and yet, I was still alive. I was conscious but dazed, more numb than in pain. *Good God, what have I done? How am I not dead?* I'd never considered that I might fail to kill myself, let alone the consequences.

I was slumped against the headboard, splattered in blood, the gun dangling from my right hand. I was too disoriented to think about shooting again. Besides, I had to answer the phone. Priorities, right? It was the hotel's landline on the nightstand to my left. I didn't care who was calling as much as I wanted the annoying ringing to stop.

"Hlllllllllll . . . ," I moaned, my best attempt at saying the word *hello* with a mangled tongue.

"Erik? It's Chris Germann! Are you listening to me? Whatever you have in your hand, please drop it now! Do you hear me, Erik? Drop what's in your hand!"

I continued moaning.

"Erik, open the door! Drop what's in your hand and open the door! Someone is coming to help you!"

Chris was two thousand miles away in New Orleans. He'd just moved his son into his new place for college. When Chris arrived at his hotel for the evening, he scrolled through his text messages and found mine. Several minutes had passed since I'd sent it: "Hey, buddy. When 911 is called, I'm at the Good Nite Inn in Calabasas. . . . Please take care of Dillon for me."

Over the next few minutes, Chris made several calls using his cell phone and the landline in his hotel room. The first call was to me on my cell, but I didn't answer. The next, he later told me, was to dispatch at the sheriff's station where he worked, which was minutes from the Good Nite Inn.

"I identified myself, told them what was happening, and asked who was working in the field that night," Chris recalled.

With the cops and paramedics on the way, Chris then called the Good Nite Inn's front desk and had them connect him to my room. That's when I picked up. Chris knew by my incoherency that he was too late to stop me—but maybe not to save me. His instinct to order me to drop what was in my hand was an educated hunch. He inferred from my text message that I was going to try to kill myself, so I probably had a weapon.

"I heard a thud," Chris recalled. "Something hit the floor."

I'd tossed the gun.

Chris then called his buddy, who was one of the officers dispatched to the scene. He'd just arrived at the hotel when Chris reached him. At some point in this chaos, I'd propped open the door with a bloody towel.

According to Chris, when his buddy first saw me, he simply uttered, "Oh my God!"

After the paramedics treated me on-site, I either walked to the ambulance under my own power or flew by helicopter to the hospital. I've heard both versions from different people, and not surprisingly, I don't know which is accurate. I recall little of what happened then and in the days, weeks, and months that followed. As I share what bits and pieces I do recall, I have also enlisted the impeccable memories of some of those close to me to fill in the gaps, including Anna Dergan.

Anna and I have been close friends since high school. To know her character, you needn't look further than her four-legged family members: about a dozen dogs at any given time, elderly ones that she adopts from owners who no longer want them. Anna is a nurturer with a giant heart replete with unconditional love. It's no surprise that she was the first person by my side in the hospital, and thank goodness she has never left it.

"Kelley called me in a panic because of a text you sent her, stating that you loved her and to hug her sons for you," Anna recently told me. "But you didn't tell her where you were. So for the first few hours, we knew nothing."

Between eleven and midnight, law enforcement contacted someone in my family to say I'd been in an accident and transported to a hospital.

"They didn't tell us what the accident was or where they took you," Anna said. "We called every hospital we could think of and checked under Erik Kramer and William Kramer (his given name). At about three in the morning, Kelley finally located you in the critical care unit at Northridge Hospital under the name William Monet."

I don't know where that name came from. As a humorous side note, when I attempted to get my medical records from the hospital a few years later, the person I spoke with said they had no records of anyone named Erik Kramer or William Kramer. I argued with them until Anna stepped in.

"Oh no," she said. "They're under William Monet."

"Monet? Why Monet?"

"You're asking me?" she laughed.

It's a mystery that likely will never be solved.

Once Kelley found me, the hospital staff told her why I was there, and she relayed that information to Anna.

"It didn't make any sense," Anna said. "Nobody had ever associated you with suicide. I'd been one of your best friends for years, and until you went for treatment in Michigan that summer, you'd never told me you were depressed. Ever. I had no idea this had been going on for so long."

Dillon had the same reaction:

"I'd noticed sometime that spring that you'd been kind of quiet. You said you'd been feeling sad and detached—like you weren't yourself," Dillon recalled. "But it didn't seem drastic at all. I knew this wasn't foreign to you. I'd heard stories about you dealing with this kind of thing during your career, but nothing about you wanting to kill yourself. It wasn't on my radar or anyone else's. Even when you said you were going to Michigan, it was like, 'Hey, I've been feeling kind of down, so I'm going to a place in Michigan to get treated.' Honestly, you talked about it as if you were going to a resort. I told you I supported you and to do what you had to do. Even years later, after going through therapy myself and recalling what happened, I don't see how I ever could've known you would do something like that."

Patrice said she felt guilty for not recognizing the severity of my condition while I was staying with her before I left for Michigan. I assured her that she couldn't have known.

"I felt like I'd failed you," Patrice remembered. "I thought there had to have been something more I could've done. But the way you acted, you sounded okay. We talked a lot about your parents and your life. I didn't see any outward symptoms of someone about to kill himself. It shows how depression works. You can have what you think is a logical and reasonable conversation with someone battling depression, and they may seem receptive when you tell them you're here for them, but there's something completely different happening in their head."

Those who haven't had depression may not comprehend why someone would conceal it, but there are plenty of reasons. We don't want to burden others. We feel like we can deal with it on our own. We fear judgment or rejection because of the stigma. We think those who've never had it won't understand. Or we just don't believe anyone can help us. Not telling Kelley or Dillon or Anna wasn't personal; it was just part of depression's ability to control how we rationalize, which is usually pretty irrational. It's fascinating and sad to recall how I noticed the huge crowd during Griffen's funeral and the outpouring of love for our family, wishing that Griffen could've seen how much people valued him. Yet, at my most critical juncture, I couldn't see the value in my own life and how much people cared for me. I have no explanation, other than that's how powerful depression is.

At about three thirty in the afternoon the next day, Anna arrived at the hospital and slipped past the staff to get to my room. Something else you should know about Anna is that she owns a successful talent agency and is a human resources consultant. So when it comes to problem-solving skills—including how to evade hospital employees to be with her friend who might be dying— nothing's going to stop her.

"You were unconscious when I walked in. It was heartbreaking," Anna recalled. "Your head was swollen bigger than a watermelon. Your left eye was drooping and was asymmetrical with the other one. Doctors didn't know yet if you were going to make it. But I always look for the positive, so I stood next to you and continually whispered, 'You're a fighter! You've *got* to keep fighting! Everybody loves you!' I needed to give you that will. I don't know if you could hear me, but I believed you could."

The next couple weeks were intense. I underwent brain surgery, but doctors had to stop midway through because of swelling so extensive that they weren't sure I would survive. They put me into a medically induced coma and on life support. A ventilator, tracheostomy tube, feeding tube, and catheter kept me alive.

"I researched brain injuries, trying to find any positive literature or videos to share with your family," Anna said. "I wanted to rally everyone around you, but it was difficult for all of us. Once the swelling went down, your forehead gradually caved in where you'd shot out part of your brain. Looking at you and the damage to your face and head, even someone as optimistic as me questioned how you could survive."

The staff at Northridge saved me with exceptional skill and patience. They safely brought me out of the coma after two and a half weeks, but I had a steep and towering mountain to climb. Physically, I had to undergo several more surgeries in the coming months, including on my skull, tongue, and jaw. Mentally, the destruction to my brain set me back a lifetime.

"You had to learn how to talk and write and walk all over again," Anna reminded me. "Your writing was scribbling, like a toddler's. And when you would write something legible, it was often the same word over and over. When you looked around the room, you'd turn your head very slowly without saying anything, taking it all in and trying to comprehend what you were seeing. And you lost a *lot* of weight. Before this, you were around two hundred pounds. At this point, you were down to about one hundred forty. The feeding tube was your only source of nutrition."

Doctors told my family that my initial recovery could take years, followed by years of rehabilitation. I was a grown man—a former NFL quarterback—reduced to having the demeanor of a child.

Anna has always referred to my suicide attempt as "an accident." I used to disagree because it was intentional, done of my own volition. But knowing now how depression manipulates the mind, her assessment is fair. I never skirt responsibility, but people need to know that who I was and am without it and who I was with it are two entirely different people. Without depression, suicide never would've crossed my mind. With it, I felt possessed by an evil spirit that caused me to dislike myself, distrust my abilities, detest the world around me, doubt that I would ever shake its grip, and go to dangerous depths, like attempting to end my life.

Now, whenever I encounter someone with depression, I repeat Dr. Wildenhaus's words: "Suicide is a permanent solution to what may be a temporary problem." Believing depression may be temporary isn't easy to do when experiencing it, which is why it's vital to know now. And if your depression insists that it's not temporary and is here to stay, as it did to me in 2015, don't believe it. Therapy, medication, natural remedies such as exercising and eating healthy, or any combination of these can be effective coping mechanisms. But a crucial step in finding hope, riding it out, and coming out the other side is convincing yourself that the depressed you is not the real you, and the real you *will* return. Hug that truth with every bit of strength you have, and don't let go.

CHAPTER 20

A NEW LOVE FOR TELEVISION

The next seven months were exhausting for Anna and Kelley, two of my guardian angels, as they and numerous medical professionals taught me how to live again.

My progress was promising at the start. At the end of September, I transferred from Northridge to the neuro-rehabilitation program at UCLA for my next stage of care. I was there for two weeks and made significant strides working with top therapists.

"They fed you soft foods as you relearned how to chew and swallow," Anna recalled. "Then you started to move around and have short conversations. Your speech was slow and your mind would drift to something else in the middle of a conversation, but at least you were talking. We reacquainted you with some of your friends, and you knew them all. You also started reacting more to your surroundings, which was fascinating to watch. For example, you would go to the mirror, remove your protective helmet, rub your hand across your caved-in forehead, and say, 'Huh, I wonder what happened there.' And then you'd put on the helmet and walk away. No more questions. No emotion whatsoever. It was good to see you questioning things, but you still had no memory of what you'd done."

UCLA is also where I was reintroduced to a technological marvel that became popular in the 1950s: the television. I had one in my room and behaved like a kid today getting his first cell phone.

"The issue with the TV was amusing and frustrating all at once," Anna said. "You acted like you'd never seen one before. You were hypnotized, particularly by a French game show you found. You didn't understand a word but the bells, music, and cheering captivated your attention."

William Monet? A French game show? Maybe I was rediscovering a past life I'd lived.

"You were so zoned out watching television that you were disinterested in everything else, including eating and sleeping," Anna continued. "Your apathy toward eating was also because you never felt hungry—your brain wasn't making a connection with your stomach. Kelley finally bribed you to eat by promising you I'd massage your neck if you did. So you would eat, I'd massage your neck, and you would fall asleep within fifteen minutes— two birds with one stone. Once the nurses realized this worked, they allowed me to come in each night after visiting hours to go through the same routine."

My next rehabilitation stint began in early October at the Centre for Neuro Skills (CNS) in the San Fernando Valley. This part of my recovery lasted for nearly four months, through January 2016. I lived in a supervised residential home and was bused to CNS each weekday for seven hours of rehab and therapy.

"The primary purpose of the home was for you to learn how to live independently—shop for groceries, do laundry, cook, and clean," Anna said. "Physically, your left side was weaker than your right, so you had to be careful not to lose your balance. But you were doing well overall. One day, several of us went to the home for a barbecue, and you did the grilling. You'd come a long way."

But my mental progress was slow.

"Your first night at CNS, you said to me, 'Anna, I know I was at Northridge and then UCLA, and now I'm here. But why was I in the hospital in the first place?' It was the first time you'd asked, which I took as a good sign. When I told you that you'd had an accident, you asked me for specifics. I said, 'Well, I'm not sure what terminology the doctors want me to use, so you should ask them in therapy tomorrow.' You said okay and happily moved on to something else. When I checked with the doctors later that week, they said you'd never asked."

My mental deficiencies were especially glaring around the television, which continued to be an addiction at CNS.

"Your favorite thing was to put the channel guide on the screen and scroll nonstop, so we would have to watch whatever program was on in that little box in the corner while you paged through the guide, sometimes for the length of an entire show," Anna said. "We couldn't get you to drop the remote long enough to go to the bathroom unless we made you. One time you were on the phone leaving a voice mail for a friend and stopped talking midsentence because something on the TV caught your eye. I had to remind you to finish your message. Another time, we were watching a football game that was coming down to the wire when you switched the channel. When we all screamed at you to turn it back, you didn't understand what you'd done. You did a lot of little things without any reason or awareness. There was an obvious disconnect between your brain and the rest of your body that posed a serious challenge."

At the start of February 2016, my insurance no longer covered my living in the supervised residential home, so I moved back home to Agoura Hills, where Anna stayed with me for two weeks and drove me to and from CNS daily.

"We gave you your phone during this time, and it became another obsession," Anna said. "You'd scroll and scroll and scroll and make us late to the clinic every morning. You had no concept of time. The one positive from this was that if I had to go to the store to get something in the evening, I could leave you home alone for a short period of time and know you'd be safe because you'd remain in the same spot on the sofa doing the same thing with your phone or the television."

But I did surprise Anna one day during those two weeks, which led to a big step in my recovery.

"I told you I had to run to Target and asked if you wanted to go," Anna said. "It was a formality to ask because you never wanted to go, but this time, you did. I noticed then as I was driving and whenever I had driven you to CNS that you paid close attention, telling me to 'watch that person' or 'be careful of that car.' So when we came out of Target, I asked if you wanted to drive us home. You said yes, and sure enough, you drove like you used to and knew how to get us home. You said you weren't ready to jump on the freeway yet, which I saw as another victory because you were aware of what you were and weren't comfortable doing and listened to yourself."

Because Anna worked full-time and couldn't continue caring for me each day, she and Kelley moved me from CNS to the Nevada Community Enrichment Program (NCEP) in Las Vegas after those two weeks. I spent eight hours there each weekday and lived with Kelley and her boys. Anna visited every other weekend, and Dillon came out every few weeks.

"The first time we saw each other in Vegas, you said, 'Hey, Dillon. How are you doing?'" Dillon recalled. "Just that you recognized me was cool, and we were able to have a nice conversation. But the next day, we go to brunch at a place with a TV in every corner, and you were locked in when you spotted a screen. Totally locked in, like nobody else was there. What was crazy was that they had nothing on but softball, and in the twenty years of my life, I'd never seen you watch a minute of softball. When I asked you why you were so interested, you said it moved fast and had a lot of action. I thought, *Okay, this is good. He's walking and talking, and the TV is stimulating his mind.* But that's also when the reality of your situation started to set in. I realized then that you were my dad and I loved you, but you would never again be the same person I used to know."

Anna felt the same way.

"Your mental development first stalled when we moved you to Vegas," Anna said. "You were doing well physically and your long-term memory was good, but your short-term memory was lacking. The biggest issue, though, was the mental connection that was still missing.

"One example is when Kelley, her sons, and I played basketball with you in ninety-five-degree weather," Anna continued. "You were wearing a sweatshirt on top of another shirt. You were soaked in sweat but insisted you weren't hot—and you truly didn't think you were because your body and brain were on separate wavelengths. When we told you to take off the sweatshirt anyway, you did. You normally listened to us, but what if nobody had been there to direct you? That's why you needed around-the-clock care. Doctors said it would probably take two to three years for you to initially recover from the traumatic brain injury, and you were only in your sixth or seventh month of rehab. But because we didn't fully understand how the brain recovers, we began to wonder if this would be as good as you would get."

Fortunately, it wouldn't. My lapse in progress at NCEP was not due to the program or even so much my television and phone obsessions. The problem, as we would all learn, was Cortney.

Cortney was a woman I'd begun dating after Griffen's death in 2011. I'd broken up with her in January 2015, seven months before I shot myself. Yet a year after our split, just before my treatment in Las Vegas, she shamelessly reinserted herself into my life. Not as a concerned friend but as a con artist who saw an opportunity to cash in.

When I finished this book, seven years after Cortney's scam came to light in October 2016, the case against her was still pending. The astonishing story of how and why this has dragged through our legal system, even after Cortney admitted her crimes to a detective a month after they were discovered, is off topic and for another time. But there are two aspects to the case that I want to share because they can happen to anyone—especially those with brain injuries or mental illness, the elderly, or anyone else in a vulnerable position.

The first is how Cortney drained money from my accounts through deception and coercion. What she did wasn't rocket science. All it took was a combination of one dishonest person and an incapacitated one.

The second is a false accusation she made against me that a simple Internet search will reveal because the media was quick to jump on it. But if you search for the result of the false charge—i.e., the truth—you won't find it because the media didn't report it. Some have said I should let it go and not discuss it. I disagree. I'm sharing it for every person who has been falsely accused of anything, especially publicly, and I thank attorney Todd

Melnik for that perspective. He's the lawyer who cleared his innocent client of murder in the 2017 Netflix documentary *Long Shot* and who eventually helped me. All of us who've been falsely accused deserve a voice and the right to clear our names.

CHAPTER 21

ASSESSING MY SUSCEPTIBILITY

I'd met Cortney once or twice through her brother, who was my friend at the time. Cortney and Marshawn were also friends, so that's how she knew Griffen. When Cortney appeared at my doorstep one morning soon after Griffen died, she reintroduced herself, offered condolences, and handed me a plate of homemade cookies, so I graciously let her in.

We had a long, heartfelt conversation about Griffen in my living room that day, and many similar meetups and chats followed in the weeks and months to come. I was sad, missing my son, and Cortney was there for me. She knew exactly what to say to lift my spirits.

As we became more acquainted, Cortney started bringing her young daughter to my home. We would have dinner, watch movies, and play games. It wasn't long before she asked me to pick up her daughter from elementary school on certain days while she was at work. I had the time and was happy to do it. Cortney and I didn't have much in common other than memories of Griffen, but that was enough to welcome her into my life when I was most vulnerable and craved companionship.

Cortney and I started dating in December 2011. We were an "on-again, off-again" couple for more than three years, similar to what Marshawn and I had—though Cortney and I weren't married and had no desire to be. We just enjoyed each other's company—except when we didn't. Each time I would break up with her, somehow we would end up back together again and start the cycle over. It was an all-too-familiar feeling.

In January 2015, a few months before my depression returned, Cortney and I were often fighting over petty matters, so I ended our onerous relationship for what I was sure would be for good. When people close to me heard about the breakup, I was surprised by how many had an opinion. Namely, that I'd made the correct decision. People said they didn't like her because they didn't trust her. I later learned from my Aunt Patrice that my mother, who, before she died, had met Cortney a few times, was one of them.

"Why didn't Mom ever say anything?" I asked.

"Because it wasn't her place, and you seemed happy," Patrice said.

That was Mom's natural maternal component shining through again. She was right—it wasn't her place to say anything. Yes, I was happy, at least some of the time. But her instinct was also correct. Anna shared Mom's sentiment when she stayed with me for those first two weeks in February 2016 and drove me to and from rehab at CNS daily.

"Right before we moved you to Vegas, Cortney started calling and texting you nonstop," Anna recently told me. "Then she came over and hung out for hours, one time until one thirty in the morning when I had to get you up early to go to CNS. I didn't know a whole lot about her, but one thing you said to me before you broke up with her was that your relationship was toxic and destructive. So why was she suddenly back in your life? It got even stranger the morning we left for Las Vegas. She stopped by with a stuffed animal and told you she'd miss you and not to stay away for too long. Something was up. When I asked you about it, you didn't know anything. To you, Cortney was just someone there, no different than Dillon, Kelley, and me."

I've been told that Cortney continued to call and text me in Las Vegas.

"Not long after you got settled in Vegas, NCEP called us to say that Cortney was disrupting your treatment with her constant calls and texts," Anna continued.

From my point of view, Cortney was on equal ground with Kelley and Anna for no other reason than she was present in my life daily. Not physically, but through my phone was good enough for me. And as Anna stated when she shared the story of me playing ball in a sweatshirt with her, Kelley, and my nephews in ninety-five-degree heat, if anyone had my attention, I listened. Cortney not only had my attention, but she had it through one of my favorite devices.

That's why I left Las Vegas on April 16, barely two months after getting there. Like just about everything else, I don't recall leaving. Or why. Anna said Cortney claimed to have found a doctor in Los Angeles that I could go to, so Cortney came on the sixteenth to drive me back home, and I said okay. It was the first time I'd seen her since I'd left Southern California. It was so illogical. She knew nothing about the extent of my injuries or my treatment plan. She didn't care about my health like Anna, Kelley, and Dillon did. But I didn't know any of that. I didn't even know I *had* a brain injury. People told me I did, but I didn't know what that meant. So if someone suggested that I could go home, why wouldn't I go?

"Cortney had your ear," Anna said. "She came to Las Vegas, told you she was driving you home, and that was it. There wasn't anything we could say to you to make you stay. At that point, you were seemingly under her control. It isn't easy seeing someone you love taken advantage of. And unfortunately, you weren't in a state of mind where you could connect the dots.

"We didn't know what Cortney was doing or would do," Anna continued. "But I strongly suspected that things were about to get much worse."

CHAPTER 22

THE SCAM

If you were to ask me how I did when I arrived home in April 2016 and in the summer months that followed, I would say I did great, even though much of it eludes my memory. I know I drove a little bit and spoke well because that's what people have told me. I even flew to Chicago for a weekend to meet with some old friends from the Bears, who watched out for me when I got there. I recall some of that trip, but not all of it. I had one setback in June—the first of four seizures over the next couple of years—but each one was attributed to me forgetting to take my medication. I was fine physically as long as I took my meds.

But that was the issue with regard to every facet of my life—"as long as. . . ." I needed continual monitoring because a critical mental component was still missing. The television and phone continued to be my best friends for most hours of the day. I had no awareness or concern of anything happening outside of whatever I was doing presently—which, of course, was usually watching TV or playing with my phone. I felt no emotional connection to anyone, including Dillon, Kelley, Anna, and Cortney.

They were people in my life like anyone else. And I continued to do whatever anyone told me, which was mostly Cortney because by then, she was living with me.

"I went over at least a couple times a week to check on you, and my suspicion grew with each visit," Anna recalled. "Cortney's clothes were in the guest room. Her hair dryer was in the bathroom. Her daughter's toys were scattered throughout the house. A dog was running around. Dishes were piled in the sink and on the counter. Nobody is as neat as you, Erik. When you use a plate or glass, you wash it immediately. You'll never find a dirty dish in your house unless someone else left it there."

I didn't invite Cortney to move in—I didn't have the capacity to even think to do something like that—but I didn't tell her no when she did. I figured if she was there, she was supposed to be there. And Anna soon noticed that Cortney was there *all* the time because Cortney wasn't working anymore. Anna also recognized that despite not having an income, Cortney was spending *a lot* of money.

"Packages from Amazon and other stores were delivered to your house daily that summer starting in June, two months after you moved back from Vegas," Anna recalled. "I looked at the labels because you never ordered anything from anywhere. Every box was addressed to Cortney."

One day in late June, Anna came over to request that I write a check to a doctor to pay for my portion of a bill that insurance didn't cover. Anna had taken care of all my mail, bills, and insurance issues when I was away being treated and continued to help me as needed after I returned home. As she went through my bills, she noticed one that was past due.

"You couldn't pay it because your checking account was overdrawn," Anna said. "That was a huge red flag because you were meticulous with your money before the brain injury. You always paid your bills on time and would spend all day reviewing charges on your credit and debit cards to confirm they were correct. As I dug deeper, I saw there were ATM withdrawals almost daily for between $300 and $700, transfers between accounts, credit card cash advances at a thousand dollars a pop, and charges for items I knew weren't yours."

The credit card charges under my name were from everywhere and for everything: gas stations, youth soccer fees, storage units, cosmetic procedures, hairstylists, cash back at grocery stores, car washes, convenience stores, hotels. I was unaware of it because I wasn't paying attention anymore. If I was overdrawn, I didn't try or care to determine why. My brain wasn't there yet, and Cortney knew it. After she drained my checking account, she accessed and used an account that had been dormant for more than four years: a memorial fund set up after Griffen's death. She had no conscience.

"I didn't confront Cortney about what I'd found because there was too much," Anna said. "Instead, I went straight to the police."

In January 2017, I attended a hearing as a result of my family filing a petition for conservatorship to protect me from Cortney's theft. During that hearing, Detective David Lingscheit testified to what he found in the fall while investigating the information Anna had presented to him.

He stated that on October 19, 2016, he interviewed Anna, who alleged that there were approximately $40,000 in unauthorized charges and debits from my bank accounts that were highly suspect. Based on that, the detective began an investigation, speaking to me on October 21 at the rehab facility I was attending. During that interview, I identified $42,000 in fraudulent activity. I told the detective I hadn't given anyone permission to make those transactions, nor did I know who had done so. However, when the detective and I reviewed the records, it became very clear to him that the transactions were connected to Cortney, although I was unable to make that connection.

As Det. Lingscheit testified what it was like examining the evidence with me, he explained that I had some deficiencies going through the records, which was concerning to him. He stated that I hadn't reviewed my bank statements, and I had no independent knowledge of anything to do with my finances.

My court-appointed attorney then asked Det. Lingscheit if he'd spoken to Cortney about his findings. He said he had.

"And she admitted to everything and has cooperated and provided all the records that he requested?" my attorney inquired.

"That's true," the detective replied.

On the evening of October 21, after the detective interviewed me earlier in the day, my friend Espo called to find out how my day went because Anna had informed him that the detective had interviewed me.

"You told Espo the detective was going to get your money back, and that was the end of the conversation because you were heading out to watch a random youth football game," Anna recalled. "It was no big deal to you because you had no concept of money or the magnitude of what Cortney had stolen from you."

It also didn't help that I was under Cortney's spell. This should've been an open-and-shut case. Instead, it became very complex.

Cortney asked me to call Det. Lingscheit to ask him not to press charges. It was like she was giving a command to a robot. On October 23, I apparently called the detective to make the request. He told me he hadn't decided on charges yet, which made Cortney nervous. That prompted her to go to the detective herself in late November and admit everything to try to gain some sympathy and mercy. The detective recommended that she move out of my house, return to work, and allow my family to provide any caregiving services I needed. Sound advice, for sure.

So what did Cortney do?

Not that.

On December 13, 2016, Cortney filed papers for us to get married.

Unbeknownst to anyone—including me—Cortney made a reservation with the Santa Barbara courthouse for a marriage ceremony. Nine days later, we went to the courthouse, and with a friend of hers as a witness, Cortney and I got married. Or, more accurately, she made me her husband.

It can be difficult to fathom, but hopefully, you understand from previous examples what my mental state was—I didn't know what it meant to get married. I knew the term *marriage* in its most basic form. But what it meant legally or financially or the appearance it would give to outsiders, I didn't have a clue. I woke up that morning, Cortney told me we were getting married, and so we did. It was that simple. It was no different than if I were a child and she'd said we were going to Disneyland, to the park, or to lunch.

On December 24, Dillon and Espo came to my house to visit for the holiday. Dillon noticed my finger right away. This is how the brief conversation went, according to what Dillon and Espo have told me:

"Dad, why are you wearing a wedding ring?" Dillon asked.

"Oh, I got married," I replied with no emotion.

"Why did you get married?" Espo asked.

"Cortney pushed the ball," I replied.

Espo and Dillon reminded me that Cortney had stolen thousands of dollars from me. Dillon said I reacted as if she'd stolen five dollars—I didn't understand the significance, nor did I have the capacity to care.

Why did Cortney want me to marry her? To the best of my knowledge today, she was afraid that Det. Lingscheit might still press charges. However, by marrying me, she muddied the waters. Even if the detective recommended that the district attorney's office pursue the charges and arrest her, why would they if I married her two months after finding out about her crimes?

That brings me back to the hearing in January 2017, where a conservatorship was ordered for my estate. During this hearing, Cortney promised the judge that she wouldn't open any more credit cards, make charges to any of my accounts, or withdraw any cash. In other words, she'd incur no more debt in my name or take any additional money from me. I went along with it because, due to my brain injury, I had no understanding what the whole conservatorship issue was about.

So Cortney and I returned home from that hearing still husband and wife—and she took her criminality to a new level.

Throughout 2017 and into 2018, the total theft rose to hundreds of thousands of dollars. Yes, even with a conservatorship in place, Cortney found ways to live a life of luxury off me while staying below the radar. It was a con job of epic proportions. It was equally a failure by so many within our judicial system who repeatedly gave the benefit of the doubt to the criminal more than they cared about protecting the victim.

My mental state during this time remained stagnant. Cortney was content letting me vegetate on the couch with my phone and television while she did whatever she wanted. My family and friends had little contact with me during that time because Cortney did everything she could to keep them away.

In late May 2018, Cortney attempted her boldest move yet by having me put a bid on a house. For a long time, she'd been talking about wanting us to get a new house. We looked at some as early as the fall of 2017, and she often told her daughter in front of me that it would happen one day, getting her daughter excited and me thinking about it. After some negotiating, the sellers accepted the offer. But because I was conserved, the purchase had to go through my conservator—who denied it in early June.

And that's when—for the first time since Cortney had reentered my life nearly two and a half years earlier—I was able to put a couple pieces together.

CHAPTER 23

CLEARING MY NAME

This is the ten-second conversation that took place in my head:

The purchase of a home Cortney wanted for us was denied.

Why?

Because I'm conserved.

Why am I conserved?

Because Cortney steals from me.

Simple, yet monumental. I hadn't been able to make connections like that since I'd shot myself. Let me be clear that I wasn't healed or cured. This was an isolated incident. I didn't suddenly process everything with such logic. I still didn't know what the word *conserved* meant other than I'd been told it was to prevent Cortney from stealing from me. I also didn't know how Cortney was stealing from me, what she was stealing, or how much, even though several people had explained it to me multiple times. I just knew that stealing was bad, and the words *Cortney* and *stealing* were now synonymous. It was a critical observation.

For the next week, I didn't speak to Cortney about it, and at the end of that week, I flew to Chicago for the annual Bears' alumni golf tournament. I didn't say good-bye to her before I left, nor did I text or call her while I was gone. When I arrived in Chicago, I met with Father Peter Armenio, a Catholic priest who was once a chaplain for the team. Father Pete and I used to talk a lot about life during my playing days.

"Erik, it's good to see you," Father Pete said as we met for dinner. "How have you been?"

"Great," I replied. "I'm getting a divorce as soon as I get home."

Maybe not the best way to start a conversation with a Catholic priest. And perhaps my tone was a little too matter-of-fact. But something I've learned about my brain injury, as I think back to the way I talked to peo-ple, is that I often spoke in very literal, unfiltered terms. Everything was black and white to me, not unlike the brain of a child, which is what doctors told my family I had after the shooting.

I returned home from Chicago a few days later in the evening and went straight to bed without speaking to Cortney, other than to say that the trip was fine when she asked. The next morning, as I was eating breakfast, I told her it was over. I wanted a divorce. She didn't take the news well.

If you ask Cortney, the police, and me what happened next, there are several inconsistencies between our sto-ries, which is usually what happens in tense situations like this. I'm not going to get into all the details of what I know to be the truth because the purpose of writing this book is to help people with their depression; it's not a tell-all drama meant to harm anyone. However, in a nutshell, and in an effort to clear my name, this is what happened:

I told Cortney I wanted a divorce because she'd been stealing from me. Despite the overwhelming evidence that the detective, Anna, and others had, Cortney insisted that she hadn't stolen anything and wouldn't accept a divorce. When I told her she needed to leave the house, she refused and said she was going to call the police, and I welcomed it. She went into another room to call them, out of my earshot, and when the police officers arrived, I kindly opened the door and greeted them. Within a minute, they arrested me for allegedly pushing her because, evidently, she'd told them on the phone that's what I'd done. There I was, the incapacitated and innocent one in handcuffs, while Cortney watched. I didn't fight it for the same reason I didn't fight anything, like leaving Las Vegas with Cortney or marrying her when she told me to. I just didn't understand. When someone told me to do something—like an officer ordering me to put my hands behind my back—I did it without question.

For the record, I did not push Cortney. Not then. Not ever. As my family, friends, and I would learn, it was all part of her sinister plan to take me for everything I had while ruining my life in the process.

Cortney's false claim resulted in me being booked and put in a cell until I could reach my conservator to bail me out. I was initially charged with a felony, but it was reduced to one count of misdemeanor battery. I spent one night in jail and the next three nights with friends before my conservator's assistant was able to retrieve some pertinent belongings from my home, including my anti-seizure medications and wallet. When I tried to get those items the day I was released from jail, Cortney refused to put them outside my house for someone else to pick up on my behalf, instead turning it into a legal hassle between our attorneys.

In the meantime, she continued to steal even more.

Recognizing a golden opportunity, during those four days after my arrest, Cortney pilfered another $18,710.44. She made charges on my credit card to Amazon, Target, Hulu, PetSmart, AT&T, Grubhub, the Lash Room, Vons supermarket, iTunes, StubHub, and Four Seasons hotels, among others. That total also included nine transfers totaling nearly $10,000 to her own PayPal account.

That's when, with Anna's help, I contacted Michael Frawley, a family law attorney, about dissolving the marriage. Not a divorce, though—an annulment, which was based on Cortney's fraud and my unsound mind when we were married. The annulment became official in January 2019, about eight months after the battery charge was filed against me.

One of my best defenses with regard to her false accusation can clearly be seen in a letter that Michael sent to Anna and me. He wrote the letter in response to an email Anna sent to him (a few months after the annulment was granted), inquiring about an offer Cortney supposedly made five months before the annulment to accept the dissolution and drop the domestic violence charge *if* I paid her. Michael confirmed in his letter that Cortney did just that:

"Anna has accurately set forth my conversation with Ms. Poser (Cortney's attorney), which was discussed at the August 9, 2018, meeting in my office," Frawley wrote. "Ms. Poser indicated that if Erik was to present a proposal which provided substantial monetary amounts to Ms. Baird, that she would settle the dissolution of marriage proceedings and would dismiss her domestic violence request."

Cortney didn't just want to be paid—she wanted "substantial monetary amounts" on top of what she'd already stolen from me.

On April 15, roughly three months after the annulment, I had a court hearing on the misdemeanor battery charge. It carried a punishment of up to six months in jail. Anna had given my criminal attorney at the time (not Michael Frawley) several hundred pages of evidence against Cortney—including many documenting the fact that she was lying about the domestic abuse claim—who still hadn't been arrested for any of her crimes. I'd made it clear to my attorney numerous times, on April 15 and in prior meetings, that I was innocent and wouldn't agree to anything—not even a single day of counseling. He didn't listen.

Before the hearing started, my attorney asked the judge and prosecutor if they could meet in the judge's chambers. I turned to look at Anna because neither of us knew what was happening. When they came out, the judge announced in open court that I would go through an eighteen-month diversion program that included fifty-two domestic violence counseling classes and eighteen months of psychiatric treatment. Once completed, the case would be dismissed. When the judge asked if I accepted those terms, my attorney leaned over to me.

"Say yes," he mumbled. "Say yes."

I didn't know what to do. Where did this come from? Why was I supposed to say yes? The court was silent. All eyes were on me as the judge waited for my answer. I was still a traumatic brain injury patient who felt like I had no choice and had to listen to my lawyer.

"Regrettably, yes," I said with confusion while staring at my attorney.

After the hearing, Anna and I followed my attorney into the lobby, and Anna lit him up.

"Why did you give in to something that never happened, especially when we know Cortney lied and you have evidence to prove her lies?" Anna yelled, with some colorful language thrown in.

My attorney seemed shocked, as if he'd done me a favor by keeping me out of jail. He also thought doing it his way would avoid media attention, which, spoiler alert, it didn't.

The next morning, I emailed my attorney and told him to rescind the agreement and asked him what my options were moving forward.

"And if going to court (a trial) is the option I choose, you will not be representing me," I stated in the email. I was going to do whatever it took to clear my name. Cortney had abused me enough. So had the legal system.

Anna helped me find a new criminal defense attorney, Todd Melnik, who took over the case about a month later.

"Todd copied the entire binder we had on Cortney—all seven hundred pages—including perjured declarations she'd filed with the court," Anna recalled. "He did what every attorney should do: took time with us, listened to us, and read and investigated the documents provided. And, as a result, he easily saw Cortney's motives and knew, without a doubt, that you were innocent."

Ten months later, the truth finally began to emerge.

On February 7, 2020, Cortney was charged with twelve felonies, including grand theft, forgery, and identity theft. Her bail was set at $670,000. According to the criminal complaint by the People of the State of California, "the pattern of related felony conduct involved the taking of, and resulted in the loss by Erik Kramer of, more than five hundred thousand dollars ($500,000) . . ."

Three days later, on February 10, Cortney was arrested.

The next day, on February 11, Todd got the misdemeanor battery charge against me dismissed.

My name had finally been cleared legally, but the damage was crushing. Numerous national news organizations reported my arrest the day it happened. Many of them followed up with a story a few days later that Cortney said she feared for her life being around me. None of them bothered to investigate her or the pending charges against her. She said I pushed her, and they accepted her lie without asking me what really happened. My reputation was tarnished to the extent that I couldn't get a high school assistant coaching job or run a football camp for kids.

And when police arrested Cortney and dropped the charge against me, no news organization reported it. It wasn't until Dan Wetzel with *Yahoo Sports* wrote a piece about me in August 2020 that people learned the real story.

There was a time when most journalists and news organizations had one goal: to get to the truth. Now, many of them use sensational headlines and stories to garner as many online clicks as possible because that's how they bring in revenue. Reporting that police arrested a former NFL quarterback for pushing a woman will make people click. Reporting that authorities dropped the false charge—not so much.

To every journalist who has written or broadcast my truth and the truth about Cortney and to those who will—thank you. And to anyone who has ever been falsely accused of anything—I'm sorry. I know what a helpless feeling it is. But never give up trying to clear your name and regain your rightful place in this world, no matter what an attorney or anyone else might tell you. I cannot erase the headlines that Cortney's false accusation created, but I can create new ones that share the real story of who I am.

Former tennis star Arthur Ashe is credited with saying, "Start where you are. Use what you have. Do what you can." I feel like I've been doing that my entire life. Trust me when I say it's sound advice.

CHAPTER 24

CTE

The Boston University CTE Center states that symptoms of chronic traumatic encephalopathy (CTE) include "memory loss, confusion, impaired judgment, impulse control problems, aggression, depression, suicidality, parkinsonism, and, eventually, progressive dementia." I've experienced a handful of them, including two new ones recently: a combination of impulse control problems and aggression, as Dillon can attest.

"You never used to have much of a temper, no worse than any other person," Dillon said to me. "But I've seen you be rude to people over trivial matters. It is what it is, and I know you're working on it, but it's something that's totally new to me."

Dillon's right, and it's posed a significant challenge for me and those close to me. People may continue to ask why I'm sharing something that's negative about myself. Well, because this is real life, and as I stated early on, I'm trying to help others. I can only do that by being candid about my situation.

My short temper or rudeness is infrequent. If we hang out together, you likely won't witness it. But I can get irritated by minor issues and display short bursts of anger that shock even me. I recognize them as they're happening, yet I don't feel like I can stop myself. I first noticed this latest behavior surface in 2020, when I would verbally snap at people close to me, and it became more frequent the following year. Since then, I've finally started to accept that CTE is the likely source. That's not an excuse, but acknowledging it is the first step toward trying to fix it.

CTE is a progressive degenerative brain disease with no known cure. It is often caused by repeated hits to the head and has become synonymous with concussions. However, it can only be diagnosed posthumously when the brain can be thoroughly examined. In February 2023, Boston University announced that researchers had "diagnosed 345 former NFL players with chronic traumatic encephalopathy (CTE) out of 376 former players studied (91.7 percent)." Symptoms range from memory loss to angry outbursts to depression to suicidal thoughts. According to a *New York Times* article on CTE, journalist Ben Shpigel reports, "a naturally occurring protein, known as tau, builds up over time in certain patterns" in brains of those with CTE. "The clumps of tau strangle brain cells, diminishing their ability to function before killing them entirely."

Safety Andre Waters, who retired in 1995 after a dozen years in the NFL with the Philadelphia Eagles and Arizona Cardinals, shot himself in the head in 2006. Reports state that tests upon his death concluded that he had the brain of an eighty-year-old with Alzheimer's. He was forty-four.

Cornerback Dave Duerson, who played for the Bears in the 1980s, took his own life in 2011 at age fifty. He shot himself in the chest after sending a text to his family asking that his brain be used for research. Doctors concluded that he had CTE.

Junior Seau, my teammate with the Chargers and one of the best linebackers to ever play, died of a self-inflicted gunshot wound to the chest in 2012 at age forty-three. Experts determined he had CTE.

Other well-known players diagnosed with it include Hall of Famers Mike Webster, Frank Gifford, and Ken Stabler. And the list of retired living players who have stated publicly that they have symptoms similar to those of CTE continues to grow: Brett Favre, Joe DeLamielleure, Tony Dorsett, Bernie Kosar, Darryl Talley, Jamal Lewis, and Leonard Marshall, just to name a few.

Until the early 2020s, I'd always claimed that I didn't have CTE. I hadn't suffered the most basic symptoms that other players had, such as headaches or memory lapses. Even today, I rarely get a headache to any degree, and my memory is sharp. Ask me about a game I played decades ago, and I'll remember most details. The only concussion I ever recall having at any level was when I played safety at Burroughs and led with my head once on a tackle, knocking myself out. But the protocols for detecting a concussion when I played weren't what they are now. Today, if a player takes a shot to the head during a game, officials can force him to go under a tent on the sidelines where a specialist will examine him to determine if he can return. In my day, nobody did anything—unless we were unconscious. Otherwise, coaches and teammates expected us to suck it up and keep playing, and we did.

In an August 2022 interview with radio personality Bubba "the Love Sponge" Clem, Brett Favre stated that he suffered *thousands* of concussions in his career.

"If you had asked me this ten years ago how many concussions I've had, I would've said three," Favre admitted. "The reason I would've said three: I thought concussions were when you get knocked out, where you black out for a period of time, [or] you don't know where you are, memory loss, dizzy. A boxer gets knocked out, [and] he tries to get up, his legs are rubber, that's a concussion.

"What we now know is concussions happen all the time," Favre continued. "You get tackled and your head hits the turf, you see the flashes of light or [hear] ringing in your ears, but you're able to play. Based on that, thousands, had to be, because every time my head hit the turf, there was ringing or stars going, flashbulbs, but I was still able to play. That's what's kind of frightening about the concussion thing. It's the ones that seem minor that do the damage."

I now believe CTE was likely a contributing factor in my depression and suicide attempt, just as I'm sure it plays a role in my heightened irritability today. By the time depression first struck in 1994, I'd been playing football for more than twenty years. Anyone who played as a kid in the 1970s or before knows how virtually useless our flimsy plastic helmets were. And the hits became progressively fiercer in high school, college, and the pros, especially as athletes got bigger and stronger.

Dillon has never wavered in his beliefs, as he recently told me:

"I have no doubt you have CTE, Dad," Dillon said. "You denied having it for a long time, and I get that. I'm sure it's scary for you to even think about. People who have CTE lose some control over themselves or likely will one day. It's like taking steps in the dark. You can't see what's coming, and that has to be terrifying. I also understand when you consider the linear fashion in which all of those horrible things happened—Griffen died, your mother died, your father was dying, I was living with my mom—it makes sense that you were depressed. But it doesn't make sense that you shot yourself. You've never been the kind of guy who would leave your son—unless circumstances beyond your control caused you to do it. I don't say that for me. It's the truth. Going through depression is one thing, but self-sabotage is completely different. It isn't like you to do something so drastic. I'm convinced CTE is why you did what you did."

When I die, if I donate my brain to science to check for CTE—which I will likely do—those I leave behind will learn if Dillon is correct, and I assume he is. But until then, I have a life to live and a moral responsibility to be the best person I can be, and I've made three admissions to myself in an effort to do that.

The first is that my outbursts are a problem, and I need to fix that piece of me, no matter the cause. Dillon's assessment that you lose some control over yourself if you have CTE is accurate, but I feel like this is an aspect of myself that I can still control. I've never known a football player to quit competing in any regard. It's not in our blood, and it's certainly never been in mine. CTE may ultimately win the game, but that doesn't mean it has to be winning throughout the game.

The second admission is that I'll need self-care forever. It's easy to lose sight of the fact that we all need ongoing self-care, especially when things seem to be good. I've been at rock bottom, so anything even remotely above that could give me a false sense of security. And it's that deception that can create an opening for depression or anger to slide in and take over. Recognizing that now, I've been under the care of a neurologist who's helped me try to manage the CTE symptoms I've experienced. I've also started seeing a therapist for the first time since 2014, and I don't expect I'll ever stop again.

The third admission is that I can't go about this challenge alone. After making the first two admissions to myself, I also made them to Anna, Dr. Wildenhaus, Dillon, Patrice, and Eric Hipple, and they dropped what they were doing to help. I've learned that no matter what we may suffer from, getting through it is like a group project. Family, friends, mental health professionals— they all have a role to play, and each is vital for our healing. A quarterback doesn't have much hope for success without an offensive line. Same with a singer without a band. Or a business owner without employees. Achieving optimal mental health is no different. But the first step toward getting that help is admitting that we need it.

When I decided in 2014 that I didn't need therapy anymore, I felt like I'd crossed the finish line. But what I've learned is that for someone with depression, a brain injury, CTE, or any combination of the three, there is no finish line. It's a constant challenge that requires continual effort because the chance of something harmful surfacing or resurfacing always lingers.

If I do have CTE, I can't prevent what it is doing or will do to my brain. But as long as I still have some control over it, I will continue to exert it in order to live the best life that I can—for me and those I encounter.

CHAPTER 25

LIVING FOR TODAY

If you and I were to have a conversation, you probably wouldn't be able to tell that I ever had a brain injury. I speak clearly. I don't think I look any different (other than older) than when I played football. And there isn't anything I can't do myself. I golf weekly. I go to the gym regularly. I read constantly. Along with some other former NFL players, I'm currently setting up a football camp for high school athletes. And I'm formulating school programs to help prevent depression from entering our young people's lives.

Anna's assessment is that I'm at 95 percent of where I was before the shooting. She says I still take a little longer to process things and will likely never be 100 percent because part of my brain is gone. After what I did to myself, I'll happily accept 95 percent for the rest of my life.

Dillon earned his college degree in 2023, and I'm amazed by and proud of what he's accomplished as he continues to pursue his dreams. I think of Griffen a lot. Not in a sad way, but as a son who made me proud for the eighteen years I had with him. Marshawn and I aren't friends, but we also aren't enemies. I think we see ourselves as the two people most connected to Dillon, who are playing separate but significant roles in his life. And I have a new girlfriend who brings me tremendous joy and has been instrumental in my recovery. Anna and I started dating after forty years as friends. It took us a while to see what was right in front of us, but I believe everything happens for a reason and in God's time, not ours.

Anna and me. *(Photo courtesy: Erik Kramer)*

Through the years, and especially since I attempted to take my life, I have come to know my God. I know God may look different to each of us who believe. For me, in the simplest terms, God is a higher power that is a force greater than myself. It's a force that teaches me how to live this life while serving the greater good. But it's up to me to listen and not rely on my own understanding. Based on all expert medical opinions, I shouldn't be alive today, but I am, and I trust there is a reason for that. By holding that belief close to my heart, I know my purpose will present itself in numerous ways and keep me in line with my higher power's vision for me.

One purpose I've recognized is to share my journey with those who can benefit from it. Some people who fail at suicide are upset that they failed. I'm thankful every morning when I wake up and my feet hit the floor. That failure was and will always be my greatest victory. I regret that I tried to kill myself. I don't regret surviving, and I don't ever shy away from telling my story. I'm not ashamed of it. I was sick beyond my control. If you still don't believe that, I suggest you continue reading other books and literature to learn more about depression. Chances are, you're close to many people who have gone through it, are going through it, and will go through it. I pray they never reach the point that I did. And it could be because of your understanding and intervention that they don't.

Some may find this hard to believe, but I haven't felt a minute of depression since I shot myself, and I hope I never will. If it does return, with the continued help of my family, friends, and medical professionals, I'll know what to do—and what not to do. I've quoted Dr. Wildenhaus's mantra before, but it's worth repeating: "Suicide is a permanent solution to what may be a temporary problem." I would take it a step further and say it's a permanent solution to what *is* a temporary problem. I don't have the credentials of Dr. Wildenhaus—I speak only from experience. Everyone's depression is different. But whether you use the words *may be* or *is*, there's hope either way. Depression hates hope. That's why we always need to hang onto it.

The late British Prime Minister Winston Churchill suffered from many bouts of debilitating depression, which he referred to as his "Black Dog." In a 1911 letter to his wife, Clementine, he described what it felt like when his depression lifted: "It is such a relief. All the colours come back into the picture."

I want my story to colorize people's lives and encourage them to share their experiences to aid others. According to the National Network of Depression Centers, two-thirds of those with depression don't seek out or get the treatment they need. Yet 80 percent of people treated for depression show signs of improvement in just four to six weeks. The more of us who share our stories, the more the tide will turn.

"It's interesting to watch the world talk about mental health in a different way today," Dr. Wildenhaus told me in a recent conversation. "People are more open about it, including athletes, musicians, and actors. But we still need to work on making it completely acceptable to talk about as a social issue. I see parallels between this and our country's history with tobacco addiction. You could once quietly encourage a smoker to stop, but it was the tremendous initiative of former US Surgeon General C. Everett Koop that made us understand the health consequences of tobacco use and realize that nicotine's addictive qualities are similar to heroin or cocaine. He did this before the country created warning labels for tobacco products and banned smoking in public places. That's how we need to tackle our mental health crisis, and it's happening. More people like you, Erik, are coming forward to tell their stories. For you to say there's a reason why you survived—a deeper meaning, even a spiritual cause—will encourage others to have the courage to seek help for themselves."

Since retiring as the GM for the Steelers, Kevin Colbert told me how he's been collaborating with retired players on transitioning to life after football.

"It's not easy for NFL players or anyone else going through a major change in life to lose their sense of identity," Kevin said. "Thankfully, the world is beginning to recognize the importance of mental health. In previous years, not just in football but in life in general, people kept those types of issues hidden. We always stressed with the Steelers that seeking help for a mental health issue is no different than seeing a trainer for a knee or ankle issue. Mental health, especially coming out of the COVID-19 pandemic, is something that supersedes athletics. It's everywhere, but it's treatable if we can get people to bring it to the surface."

A national sign of hope involving our youth occurred during the 2022 Little League World Series tournament, when a batter was hit in the head by a pitch. He was uninjured and jogged to first base. But when he got there, he noticed that the pitcher was crying because of the beanball he'd thrown. In a move I've never seen before at any level, the batter walked to the mound, hugged the pitcher, and told him it was okay. A video of this went viral as people praised the compassion of the batter. But I saw something more. I saw a kid who understood in real time that the mental health of the pitcher was as important as his own physical well-being. If we keep teaching our kids this way and behave this way ourselves, we will move mountains.

One lesson I've learned about depression is that there isn't a one-size-fits-all solution. We're all wired differently, we've had different life experiences, and we grew up in different environments, which is why the more tools we have to combat depression, the better chance we have of defeating it.

For me, therapy is at the top of the list. I know it can be intimidating because of the stigma. If you feel that way, I suggest starting small by having a conversation with a trusted friend or finding an online support group. But know that there are many people out there who make a living listening to what you have to say. They have big hearts and want to help people in your position. There's likely nothing you can tell them that they haven't heard from someone else. You are unique, but your problems aren't. Everybody is going through something.

Dillon can vouch for the benefits of therapy firsthand.

"I got very used to therapy at an early age because I saw you and Mom going to it when you had your issues," Dillon told me. "I went when you first split because I was overeating and crying and sad all the time. I didn't go regularly, but enough to help me get through some things. I went back when I was around twelve or thirteen, when you guys were divorcing, and after Griffen died, I started going weekly. I've never had a bad experience in therapy, and I don't understand why there's such a stigma attached to it. To me, therapy is cool. It gives you ideas and perspectives on how to deal with things. How can that not be good for someone?"

I'm also a proponent of antidepressants. Whether they're a long-term solution for you is between you and your doctor. For me, I used them as a short-term fix to help level the playing field in my mind as I tried to work my way through what I was feeling.

Another tool is removing toxicities from your life and adding what brings value and happiness. That can mean eliminating food that isn't good for you and replacing it with healthy choices, kicking bad habits like smoking and using that time to exercise, or distancing yourself from negative people and instead welcoming those who put a smile on your face. In conjunction with that, it can also mean lessening your presence on social media. Numerous studies have linked an increase in depression with increased social media use. Social media often portrays everyone's life as being great but your own, and it's human nature to compare ourselves with others. But what you see on social media sites is an artificial perception of what life is really about. Lessening your time spent on them can boost your mental health by affording you more time to make better in-person connections with those you want to be with.

One more valuable tool is the National Suicide Prevention Lifeline, which is now known as the 988 Suicide & Crisis Lifeline. When you call or text 988 or use chat services at suicidepreventionlifeline.org, a trained counselor—who can, will, and wants to help you—will answer and provide you with guidance, support, and resources.

I want to end this chapter with a story that Bill Keenist, the former director of PR for the Lions, recently reminded me of:

"My oldest son, Billy, was five years old in 1993 and loved you. I sometimes took Billy and my younger son, Chris, to work with me, so they got to know a lot of the players, and you were, by far, Billy's favorite. At the end of that season, you signed with the Bears. While I was upset to see you go, I was even more concerned with how Billy would handle it. When I got home from work and told Billy, he was devastated. He went into his bedroom and sobbed. The kid was absolutely heartbroken, and there wasn't anything I could say to make him feel better. But then the phone rang.

"'Hello?' I said.

"'Hey, Bill, it's Erik Kramer.'

"'Hey, Erik. What's up?' I'd just seen you at the Silverdome and didn't know why you'd be calling.

"'Is Billy there?' you asked.

"'Billy?'

"'Yeah, can I talk to him?'

"Imagine being five years old and getting a phone call from an NFL quarterback. You had signed a lucrative contract with a new team, yet you cared enough to call a five-year-old kid because you didn't want the kid to be sad."

I hesitated to include that story because it can come across as self-serving. But hopefully, you know me well enough now to know that's not my intent. I share it to show that while we should celebrate our victories and feel no shame for being happy, there's always someone struggling who could use our help or attention, whether it be through a text, a phone call, an invitation, or simply a kind word.

One way to collectively beat depression is to give each other hope. Look out for one another and care for each other. You never know whose spirits you may boost or life you may save.

CHAPTER 26

DEAR DILLON, PART TWO

Dear Dillon,

It seems like a lifetime ago since I wrote a goodbye letter to you and proceeded to take a step I'll never take again. Having just read that letter, it doesn't sound anything like me.

As you know, I've battled depression on several occasions. We've also discussed possible contributing factors that might've led me into that state. Now that some significant time has passed, I can confidently say that I never expect to find myself in that vulnerable position again. But if somehow I slip, I have good people close to me who are attuned to my inner workings. I'm also comfortable reaching out for help to those same few rather than internalizing my misperceptions.

These last several years have renewed my love for people, internal growth, contributing to society, and new challenges and experiences. I go to bed each night looking forward to the next day. You and Griffen have always been the most important and influential people in my life . . . and always will be. Watching you grow and mature into a man continues to make me a proud papa.

Dillon and me at Patrice's home. *(Photo courtesy: Erik Kramer)*

I admire you for engrossing yourself in positive endeavors like baseball, school, good friends, and healthy choices. I've noticed over the years that you have a small circle of friends who you've chosen wisely and carefully. Those same people will always have your back, and I know you will always have theirs.

I consider myself a fortunate man, Dillon. Not only am I still here, but I'm blessed with you as a son and have other close relationships with family and friends that I continually cultivate and grow from within. Part of what I love is seeing where you'll go in your life, how my life expands, and how we both influence others in positive ways. Life's choices aren't often easy. However, loving our way through each day brings us in contact with extraordinary people who give our journey more depth.

A past doctor of mine said several years ago that I should play the lottery every week for the rest of my life, implying that I was the luckiest man alive. What he didn't know was that with you and many others in my life, I win it every day.

I hope that over these last several years, you have come to feel that I'm no longer someone you have to worry about. There's never going to come a day when you'll have to read another goodbye letter from me. For me, the best part of every day is when my feet hit the floor each morning. I've never been more comfortable in my skin than I am now. I have a quiet confidence about me that feels very familiar and deeply rooted. While depression has been present several times in my life, inner peace has too—more so, in fact. As I've mentioned to you, many good things are going to take place over the next several months and years. Your job from here on is to live your life in the same caring and loving way that you always have. And know that I'll be doing the same.

Even though tragic events and losses have rear-ended our lives, our capacity to engage with others has grown deeper and broader. You and I are wiser because of those experiences. Together, let's keep moving forward in that lane.

I will always love you, Dillon.

Dad

ACKNOWLEDGMENTS

Countless people over many years—doctors, nurses, medical technicians, physical therapists, mental health professionals, friends, and family—have saved me and helped me regain a sense of normalcy. I will never recall all of your names. In some cases, depending on my state of mind at the time, I may not even know you were involved. But please know that I am eternally grateful to you. Because of you, I'm alive and flourishing today.

Above all, I want to thank Dillon, Patrice, and Anna for being by my side during the most difficult stretch of my life. Your love then and today is my most potent medication. And to Kelley, thank you for stepping in and handling my affairs in my vulnerable state and most significant time of need.

Special thanks to Dr. Kevin Wildenhaus for showing me that the mind is as important as the body. You transformed my career and my life. I wouldn't be here without you.

Eric Hipple, Bill Keenist, Robert Espinoza, Chris Germann, Kevin Colbert, and June Jones—thank you for your contributions to this book and my life. I will always hold your friendships close to my heart.

Todd Melnik, thank you for reviewing the facts of the case and believing in my innocence. And thank you Eileen Thompson Ray, Faith Inman, Scott Yoffe, and Dave Sturgis for your insights and hard work in making this a success.

Thank you, Bill Croyle—what patience and insight you have as both a listener and writer. As my trust in you grew, you delivered in ways I couldn't have envisioned. I truly appreciate our relationship.

Jennifer Huston Schaeffer of White Dog Editorial Services, photographer Karen Quincy Loberg, and Alan Dino Hebel and Ian Koviak of BookDesigners.com—your talents are unmatched. Thank you for your time, dedication, and friendship throughout this process.

To Alison Setters, Angie Stewart, Angie Ziegelmeyer, Carolyn Zilinski, Chris Tracey, Helen Lambron, Leslie Hughes, Lisa Kovach, and Rory Glynn, your invaluable input made this a better book. Thank you for your insight, honesty, and effort.

Thank you to the Detroit Lions and Chicago Bears for all your contributions and support with this project.

To those who endorsed this book and helped me secure endorsements for it—I am forever grateful for your kind words and continued support in my journey.

And to you, the readers—I hope I've helped you in some way. May you and everyone you love find peace and happiness in your lives.

NOTES

Chapter 9

Kevin Wildenhaus, PhD, in discussion with the author, July 2022.

Chapter 10

David Aldridge, "Lions Lose Peete but Beat Cowboys, 34–10," *Washington Post* (Washington, DC), October 28, 1991.

Eric Woodyard, "25 Years Later, Former Lion Mike Utley Won't Be Defeated by Spinal Cord Injury," *MLive*, October 24, 2016, www.mlive.com/sports/flint/2016/10/25_years_later_former_lion_mik.html.

Bill Keenist, in discussion with the author, July 2022.

Kevin Colbert, in discussion with the author, July 2022.

NFL on YouTube, "Lions Capture First Postseason Win Since 1957 | 1991 Divisional Playoffs | NFL Full Game," YouTube, January 5, 1992, video, 5:48, https://youtu.be/soH33XuFUk0.

Don Pierson, "Erik Kramer? Yes, But It's Become Kramer!" *Chicago Tribune* (Chicago), January 8, 1992, https://www.chicagotribune.com/news/ct-xpm-1992-01-08-9201030110-story.html.

Chapter 11

Rick Telander, "The Rarest of Roars," *Sports Illustrated*, January 13, 1992, 24–26.

Chapter 12

Kevin Colbert, in discussion with the author, July 2022.

Fred Mitchell, "Injured Kramer Hopes to Face Jets," *Chicago Tribune*, September 20, 1994, https://www.chicagotribune.com/news/ct-xpm-1994-09-20-9409200100-story.html.

Chapter 13

"What Is Depression?" American Psychiatric Association, accessed September 6, 2023, https://www.psychiatry.org/patients-families/depression/what-is-depression.

Chapter 14

Kevin Wildenhaus, PhD, in discussion with the author, July 2022.

Chapter 15

Sam Smith, "Pippen Still Battling a Curse that Has
Haunted Him," *Chicago Tribune*, May 24, 1991, https://
www.chicagotribune.com/sports/bulls/ct-chica-
go-bulls-scottie-pippen-headache-20200425-63n7ca5f-
w5dlpbldahug54v7ye-story.html.

Chapter 16

Robert Espinoza, in discussion with the author, July 2022.

Dillon Kramer, in discussion with the author, July 2022.

Stephanie Bertholdo, "No Jail Time for Teen
Charged in Kramer Death," *Thousand Oaks Acorn*,
November 15, 2012, https://www.toacorn.com/articles/
no-jail-time-for-teen-charged-in-kramer-death.

Chapter 18

Patrice Camron, in discussion with the author, July 2022.

Eric Hipple, in discussion with the author, July 2022.

Chapter 19

Chris Germann, in discussion with the author, July 2022.

Anna Dergan, in discussion with the author, July 2022.

Dillon Kramer, in discussion with the author, July 2022.

Patrice Camron, in discussion with the author, July 2022

Chapter 20

Anna Dergan, in discussion with the author, July 2022.

Dillon Kramer, in discussion with the author, July 2022.

Chapter 21

Anna Dergan, in discussion with the author, July 2022.

Chapter 22

Anna Dergan, in discussion with the author, July 2022.

Erik W. Kramer Conservatorship, Case No. 16STPB07356, Department No. 11, Reporter Paula B. Renteria (Superior Court of California, County of Los Angeles, January 10, 2017).

Chapter 23

Michael Frawley, letter to Erik Kramer and Anna Dergan, April 16, 2019.

Erik Kramer, email message to his attorney, April 16, 2019.

Anna Dergan, in discussion with the author, July 2022.

People of the State of California v. Cortney Baird, Rev. 920-6/03, DA Case 39049043, Case No. BA485109 (Superior Court of California, County of Los Angeles, February 7, 2020).

Chapter 24

"Frequently Asked Questions About CTE," Boston University CTE Center, accessed August 15, 2023, https://www.bu.edu/cte/about/frequently-asked-questions/#:~:text=The%20symptoms%20of%20CTE%20include,end%20of%20active%20athletic%20involvement.

Dillon Kramer, in discussion with the author, July 2022.

"Researchers Find CTE in 345 of 376 Former NFL Players Studied," Boston University Chobanian & Avedisian School of Medicine, February 6, 2023, https://www.bumc.bu.edu/camed/2023/02/06/researchers-find-cte-in-345-of-376-former-nfl-players-studied.

Ben Shpigel, "What to Know About C.T.E. in Football," *New York Times*, July 5, 2022, https://www.nytimes.com/article/cte-definition-nfl.html.

Bubba Clem, "The Untold Truth of Brett Favre's NFL Career," August 2022, *The Bubba Army Podcast*, https://www.youtube.com/watch?v=bfR8CQzmcdg.

Chapter 25

Winston Churchill and Clementine Churchill, *Speaking for Themselves: The Personal Letters of Winston and Clementine Churchill*, ed. Mary Soames (London: Black Swan Books, 1999), 53.

Kevin Wildenhaus, PhD, in discussion with the author, July 2022.

Kevin Colbert, in discussion with the author, July 2022.

Dillon Kramer, in discussion with the author, July 2022.

Bill Keenist, in discussion with the author, July 2022.

ABOUT ERIK KRAMER

Erik Kramer was the 1986 ACC Player of the Year for the North Carolina State Wolfpack and an NFL quarterback for eleven years with the Atlanta Falcons, Detroit Lions, Chicago Bears, and San Diego Chargers. Erik led the Lions to the NFC Championship Game in the 1991–92 season; the team finished one victory shy of making it to Super Bowl XXVI. He still holds several team passing records with the Falcons and Bears.

Erik is the father of Dillon and Griffen and lives in Agoura Hills, California. He enjoys reading, golfing, traveling, coaching football, and sharing his story with people young and old to help them overcome depression and other challenges in their lives.

You can follow Erik and learn more about his life and mission on X (formerly Twitter) via @EKPass or on Facebook at facebook.com/erik.kramer.505.

ABOUT WILLIAM CROYLE

William Croyle is a native of Cleveland, Ohio, and a graduate of St. Ignatius High School and Ashland University. He and his wife, Debra, live in Erlanger, Kentucky. They have three sons—Nick, Dominic, and Vincent.

William is a former journalist for the *Cincinnati Enquirer* newspaper and the author of thirteen nonfiction books written with and about some of the world's most inspirational people, including a school shooting survivor, a young mother with stage four cancer, and the last person found alive beneath the World Trade Center rubble after 9/11. You can read more about his books at www.williamcroyle.com or facebook.com/williamcroylebooks.

Made in United States
North Haven, CT
05 January 2024

47037055R10137